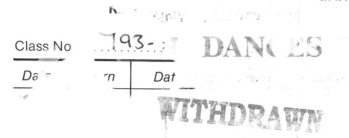

IRISH DANCES

WITHDRAWN

a collection of

TEN TRADITIONAL SETS

collected & edited by

TERRY MOYLAN

with a preface by

Breandán Breathnach

Second Edition July 1985
Reprinted in July 1987
Reprinted in May 1988

First Published 1984 in Dublin by
NA PIOBAIRI UILLEANN
15 Henrietta Street, Dublin 1.

ISBN 0 9509743 1 5

Cover picture: Dan O'Connell & Kathleen Moylan
dancing in Scartaglen, August 1983.

Co⬛⬛⬛⬛⬛⬛⬛⬛uett

⬛⬛alsh

This work is dedicated

with affection and gratitude to

The Crusheen Set Dancers

iii

Acknowledgements

Thanks are due to the following who contributed to the production of this booklet: to Joe and Siobhan O'Donovan of Cork, the most generous and unstinting sources of assistance and encouragement to anyone interested in Irish dances; to the various dancers named in the introduction to each set from whom the dances were learned; to my wife Kay and to Mary-Clare Breathnach and Janice Murphy for assistance in preparing the material for publication; to Na Piobairi Uilleann for providing space to run our dance class; and to the following, the past and present members of Brooks' Academy without whose company and enthusiasm the whole business could never have gotten started: Eadaoin Breathnach, Patsy Broderick, Gemma Brolly, Marie Brown, Margaret Byrnes, Dot Callery, Phil Callery, Mary Casey, Roma Casey, Marion Cavanagh, Genevieve Clement, Marie Colgan, Ted Colgan, Agnes Cogan, Pat Coleman, Joe Corr, Eibhlis Cramer, Eamonn Curran, Maire Delaney, Jon Dermody, Sean Donnelly, Vera Doyle, Marie Eagleton, Marian Egan, Susan Finn, Maria Fitzgibbon, Shay Fogarty, Betty Freeman, Mary Friel, Derbhil Galldubh, Mary Gleeson, Maria Goodwin, Bernie Grehan, Claire Grehan, Jimmy Grehan, Nuala Hand, Dick Hogan, Breda Holly, P.J. Howell, Jeff Kallen, Breda Kennedy, Sean Kilkenny, Cait Maguire, Ann Mahoney, Cormac Maloney, Oliver Maloney, Siobhan Maloney, Brid Manifold, Irene Martin, Ann Meade, Carol Meade, Noel Maloney, Enda Mooney, Michael Moran, Pat Moroney, Kathleen Moylan, Aideen Mulcahy, Angela Murray, Avril Murray, Mary Murray, Michael Murray, Caroline McCamley, Betty McCoy, Emer McManus, Edel McWeeney, Bernie Normoyle, Noel Normoyle, Pat O'Connell, Patricia O'Connor, Mary O'Dwyer, Antaine O'Farachain, Terry O'Friel, Esther O'Hanlon, Greg O'Hanlon, Phil O'Meara, Anne O'Reilly, Jerry O'Reilly, Rhona Preston, Eamonn Quigley, Huguette Rabault, Ann Relihan, Anne Reynolds, Kitty Russell, Bridget Ryan, Connie Ryan, Aidan Scanlon, Jackie Small, Tricia Somerville, Anne Stafford, Margaret Taylor, Maeve Toner, Mary Turley, Aidan Vaughan, Margaret Whelan and Geraldine Williams.

Contents

Preface

For the past half century or more almost all of the dance music played by traditional performers and especially by pipers, was played for listening to rather than for dancing. So common had this odd situation become that some musicians openly displayed their annoyance when, striking up to play, people in their company took the floor to dance. The compliment was lost upon these musicians.

What seems to be a return to the proper order of things has resulted from the work of the Willie Clancy Summer School. This week-long course in traditional music and song, held to perpetuate the memory of Willie Clancy, a founder member of Na Píobairí Uilleann, included the dancing of sets in its programme for the first time in 1982. The class was conducted by Joe O'Donovan whose enthusiasm for the art was infectious and pipers who attended because they had nothing else to do experienced for the first time the exhilaration of the dance.

The urge once awakened was not to be satisfied by an annual visit to Miltown Malbay and means were sought to practise and perfect on a regular basis throughout the year what had been taught during the School. The Council of Na Píobairí Uilleann were delighted to provide the necessary accommodation at their headquarters in 15 Henrietta Street. Dancing is now a regular activity and it is not at all uncommon to have four or five full sets on the floor together on Monday nights there. The initial enthusiasm has been sustained since Joe O'Donovan, whose business took him on a monthly visit from Cork to Dublin, with characteristic generosity fitted in a class, continuing where he had left off in Miltown.

The sets, and the quadrilles from which they were derived had long since ceased being danced in Dublin and indeed throughout the countryside. Here and there local forms survived and when word was got of such a friendly visit was arranged, to join in the dancing and with the hosts' agreement to add the set to the pipers' repertoire.

Terry Moylan, the guiding spirit in this exploration has gathered the result of these travels in IRISH DANCES. The ten dances from places as far apart as Sliabh Luachra and Monaghan are set down in this guide not to fix their form rigidly but to serve as a framework in which people may the more easily and quickly acquire the figures and movements of these local sets.

This work offers an opportunity to those interested to share in an enthusiasm and to experience the exhilaration of the dance. It is besides a practical way of expressing our gratitude to those people who each year undertake the burden of organising the Willie Clancy Summer School, to Joe O'Donovan for the tremendous work he put into teaching these dances, and of acknowledging the generosity of those groups who had preserved and shared their heritage of dancing.

Na Piobairi Uilleann are pleased to play a part in this movement and in placing IRISH DANCES before the public are certain that the association once more of dance and music augurs nothing but good for the future.

BREANDÁN BREATHNACH
Chairman,
Na Piobairi Uilleann.

Introduction

In 1982, for the first time, the teaching of set dances was included as one of the activities of the Willie Clancy Summer School. After spending the week learning the Kerry Set and other dances under the guidance of Joe O'Donovan, I and a couple of others did not want to leave it at that but returned to Dublin intent on setting up a class or club to continue the learning of sets. An offer of space in which to conduct a class at the premises of Na Piobairi Uilleann was availed of, and in the autumn of 1982 a club-cum-class was started.

The class has tried to operate on co-operative lines, with members travelling out to visit other groups to learn sets and then bringing them back and teaching the rest of the class. Generally, anyone knowing a set has shared their knowledge. In this way seventeen dances have been learned, including eleven sets. A difficulty felt from the start was the lack of any readily available manual for use in teaching the dances. So far as could be established only two works giving instructions for Irish dances have been published in this century, one around 1911, and one in the fifties, and both deal with the ceili and figure dances and have nothing to say about sets. This despite the fact that they are danced all over the country and have been for nearly two hundred years.

Therefore, "since the wise have not spoken, ...", in the absence of any existing tutor we have been obliged, with the assistance of Na Piobairi Uilleann, to bring out our own. Originally intended as just a stapled collection of instruction sheets for distribution to students it has expanded in size and scope, and in the size of its intended audience, as other aspects of the subject seemed to call out for inclusion, and as we became more aware of the need for such a manual.

It is aimed at those who would teach the sets, and those who would learn them. It does not purport in any way to be a definitive account of the subject, but it is hoped that it will prove useful as an aid for those engaged in promoting the dances. Probably city and town dwellers for the most part might benefit from it, for many areas of the countryside still preserve the practise of dancing sets as a normal social activity. For people lucky enough to live in such areas this book should have merely academic interest.

It must be emphasised that the descriptions of dances which follow are not presented as being definitive or ideal descriptions. They are merely versions, collected from particular sources and sometimes co-existing with several other more or less similar versions within relatively small areas. The versions here are those that happened to be encountered first by the organisers of the set-dance club referred to above. No attempt has been made to check them against other versions, or to establish whether or not they represent each set in its most "authentic" form. The source of each set is given, and it may be taken that the following pages contain as full and accurate a description as the writer could achieve of the sets as they are danced in the areas mentioned. Those who are privileged to be living in an area where the tradition still lives are urged not to use these versions as standards against which to judge their own dances, or to change their own dances to conform to the versions here. On the contrary, I would be most interested to hear of other versions of the sets presented here, and of other sets.

Recently the club/class already referred to has appropriated to itself the title "Brooks' Academy". No considerations other than the need for a good name influenced the choice of that title. However, the linking of our club with a nineteenth century school of dance is symbolic of one thing in that it reflects the fact that the attitude of the organisers towards the dances is hopefully the same as that of our nineteenth century predecessors - acknowledgement and acceptance of the origins of the dances, and unconcern with artificial divisions between one form of social entertainment and another based upon someone's declaration that one is "traditional" and another is not. It is hoped that all who buy this book will go on to dance the sets simply because they are enjoyable for their own sake. When danced well they afford pleasure to dancer and onlooker alike. It is hoped also that the publication of this collection will help to restore the dancing of sets as a widely accepted form of entertainment. I look forward to the time when as many firms engage ceili bands as rock groups for their Christmas parties, and when at least one public house in every parish is known as a place where sets are danced.

A word of explanation on the terminology employed in the instructions may not be out of place. Some of the movements common to several sets bear different names in different areas. Consistency demanded that the same term be applied to the same movement wherever it occurs. Consequently, wherever there were different terms for the same movement the most commonly used one has been employed here. Also as there are two views as to the positions of 1st sides couple and 2nd sides couple relative to 1st tops couple, the most generally accepted orientation, as encountered by the writer, has been adopted for use here.

The music for the various figures must be played at a speed that the dancers find comfortable, and it can be played too slow as well as too fast for comfort. The following tempos have been found to be satisfactory, the more experienced dancers preferring the faster end of the range:

	Reel	Jig	Hornpipe	Polka	Slide
BARS PER MINUTE:	58-62	58-62	46-50	66-70	66-70
METRONOME: (2 beats per bar)	116-124	116-124	92-100	132-140	132-140

The number of bars to be found at the top of each figure indicates the number of bars required to dance all the movements, together with the eight bars that are usually let go by before the dancing starts.

TERRY MOYLAN

Preface to the Second Edition

The printing of a second edition has provided an opportunity to correct errors which, in spite of several checks of the proofs, crept into the first edition. These occurred in the Caledonian set - figure 5 (B(i)), and in the Castle set - figures 5 (J), and 6 (F, G and H). The opportunity has also been availed of to introduce alterations to certain of the figures where it has seemed to us that such changes would make those figures conform more closely to traditional practise. These changes are as follows. On the advice of Aidan Vaughan, of Clare, figures 3 and 4 of the Plain set have been switched, and in figure 3 here, (figure 4 in the first edition), the ladies rather than the gents cross first in the figure. In the Castle set alterations have been made to figures 3 and 5, on the recommendation of Connie Ryan, from whom the set was originally learned. Comparison of the corrected and/or altered versions here with the versions in the first edition will reveal all the changes to those interested.

It is no harm to note that errors in the transmission of information provide the mechanism whereby new versions (or species) of everything arise, from dances to ducks, and variety has ever been the spice of life. Keep on dancing.

TERRY MOYLAN

The Kerry Set

LEARNED IN MILTOWN MALBAY FROM JOE
O'DONOVAN.

THE KERRY SET

'Hands Around'

Polka - 152 bars

Opening Position: Couples adopt the standard position. (see page 81)

A <u>BODY</u>	All couples dance together one bar into the centre and one bar back to their own positions.	
	They then dance two bars around to the position of the couple to their right, turning clockwise as they go.	
	The four couples repeat this movement three more times until they end up back in their original starting positions.	16 bars
B <u>FIGURE</u> (a)	<u>HANDS AROUND:</u> The four dancers of the 1ST TOPS & 2ND TOPS join hands in the centre and wheel around clockwise (4 bars), then turn, join left hands in the centre and wheel anti-clockwise back to their starting positions, (4 bars). (see page 82)	8 bars
(b)	<u>SWING:</u> TOP COUPLES swing in place.	8 bars
C <u>BODY</u>	All four couples dance the Body, as above.	16 bars
D <u>FIGURE</u>	SIDE COUPLES repeat B.	16 bars
E <u>BODY</u>	All four couples dance the Body, as above.	16 bars
F <u>FIGURE</u>	TOP COUPLES repeat B.	16 bars
G <u>BODY</u>	All four couples dance the Body, as above.	16 bars
H <u>FIGURE</u>	SIDE COUPLES repeat B.	16 bars
I <u>BODY</u>	All four couples dance the Body, as above.	16 bars

THE KERRY SET

'House And Home'

Opening Position: Couples adopt the standard position.

A <u>BODY</u>	All four couples dance the Body as in Figure 1.	16 bars
B <u>FIGURE</u>	(a) <u>HOUSE:</u> 1ST TOPS dance around the house inside.	8 bars
	(b) <u>HOME:</u> 1ST TOPS side step into the centre (1 bar) and dance on the spot (1 bar), side step back to their position (1 bar) and dance on the spot, (1 bar). They then dance around at home (4 bars).	8 bars
C <u>BODY</u>	All four couples dance the Body.	16 bars
D <u>FIGURE</u>	1ST SIDES repeat B.	16 bars
E <u>BODY</u>	All four couples dance the Body.	16 bars
F <u>FIGURE</u>	2ND TOPS repeat B.	16 bars
G <u>BODY</u>	All four couples dance the Body.	16 bars
H <u>FIGURE</u>	2ND SIDES repeat B.	16 bars
I BODY	All four couples dance the Body.	16 bars

'Slide'

3rd Figure

Slide - 184 bars

Opening Position: Couples adopt the standard positon.

A	BODY	All four couples dance the Body as in Figure 1.	16 bars

B FIGURE (a) SLIDE: TOP COUPLES side step towards each other in the centre (2 bars), and then side step back to their own positions (2 bars).

4 bars

(b) CHANGE: TOP COUPLES dance half-way around the house to each other's position.

4 bars

(c) SLIDE: TOP COUPLES repeat (a).

4 bars

(d) CHANGE: TOP COUPLES repeat (b) to bring them back to their original positions again.

4 bars

(e) HOUSE: TOP COUPLES dance around the house inside.

8 bars

C BODY   All four couples dance the Body.

16 bars

D FIGURE   SIDE COUPLES repeat B.

24 bars

E BODY   All four couples dance the Body.

16 bars

F FIGURE   TOP COUPLES repeat B.

24 bars

G BODY   All four couples dance the Body.

16 bars

H FIGURE   SIDE COUPLES repeat B.

24 bars

I BODY   All four couples dance the Body.

16 bars

4

'Ladies Right Hands In'

4th Figure   Polka - 88 bars

Opening Position: Couples adopt the standard position.

A BODY   All four couples dance the Body as in Figure 1.   16 bars

B FIGURE   (a) LADIES RIGHT HAND IN: The four ladies join right hands in the
                centre and wheel clockwise half-way around to the opposite gents.

                Each lady joins left hands with the opposite gents left hands and
                turns clockwise under his left arm, dances around behind him and
                comes back in again on his right side.

                The four ladies again join right hands in the centre and wheel
                clockwise back to their own partners.   8 bars

             (b) SWING: All four couples swing in place.   8 bars

C BODY   All four couples dance the Body.   16 bars

D FIGURE   Repeat B.   16 bars

E BODY   All four couples dance the Body.   16 bars

'Change Partners'

5th Figure   Hornpipe - 128 bars

Opening Position: Couples adopt the standard position.

A BODY	All four couples dance the body as in Figure 1, to the hornpipe step.	
	As the couples dance to the centre, instead of hopping to commence the bar that will bring them out again they stamp instead, ladies with the left foot, and gents with the right.	16 bars
B HOUSE	All four couples dance house around.	8 bars
C CHANGE & BODY	The Body is danced again, as above, but with a change of partner.	
	For the first two bars the gents dance in and out on their own, while the ladies dance around to the next position as they would if they were dancing around the house with their partners.	
	When the gents dance back out again they join up with the new partners and complete the body with them.	16 bars
D HOUSE	All four couples dance house around.	8 bars
E CHANGE & BODY	Repeat C.	
	The ladies move one place around again.	16 bars
F HOUSE	All four couples dance house around.	8 bars
G CHANGE & BODY	Repeat C.	
	The ladies move one place around again.	16 bars
H HOUSE	All four couples dance house around.	8 bars
I CHANGE & BODY	Repeat C.	
	The ladies move one place around again to rejoin their original partners.	16 bars
J HOUSE	All four couples dance house around, doubling the last two bars.	8 bars

The Monaghan Set

LEARNED IN DUBLIN FROM JOE O'DONOVAN WHO RECONSTRUCTED IT WITH THE HELP OF ED SWEENEY OF CLONES, CO. MONAGHAN.

THE MONAGHAN SET IS EXCEPTIONAL AMONG THE SETS PRESENTED HERE IN ITS USE OF FOUR DIFFERENT DANCE MEASURES.

THE MONAGHAN SET

'Wheel & Ladies Chain'

═══

Opening Position:	Couples face anti-clockwise around the circle, gents on the inside. Each gent holds his partner's left hand in his left hand, and with his right arm over the lady's shoulder holds her right hand in his right hand. (see page 82)	
A LEAD AROUND	(a) All four couples dance anti-clockwise around until they reach their own positions. On the last bar the four couples turn in place to face clockwise. They turn clockwise, out of the circle, without letting go hands. Gents remain on the inside of the circle but with left arms over the ladies shoulders.	
	Partners should not turn around each other, each dancer turns on the spot.	8 bars
	(b) All four couples dance clockwise back around to their own places again.	
	On the last bar the gents release their partners left hands, take the ladies right hands with their left hands and adopt the standard position.	8 bars
B HOUSE	All four couples dance house around.	8 bars
C HOME	All four couples dance around at home.	8 bars
D FIGURE	LADIES RIGHT HAND CHAIN: The four ladies dance around inside the circle in a chain.	
	To commence the top ladies give their right hands across their bodies to the ladies on their left, and side ladies give their right hands out to the ladies on their right.	
	Top ladies never touch each other, nor do side ladies.	8 bars
E SWING	When the four ladies rejoin their partners all four couples swing in place.	8 bars
F LEAD AROUND	Repeat A.	16 bars
G HOUSE	All four couples dance house around.	8 bars
H HOME	All four couples dance around at home.	8 bars
I FIGURE	LADIES LEFT HAND CHAIN: Repeat D as above, but substituting left for right, and vice versa.	8 bars
J SWING	When the four ladies rejoin their partners all four couples swing in place.	8 bars

THE MONAGHAN SET

'Crossover'

Jig - 128 bars

Opening Position: All dancers face to centre, joining hands in a circle.

A	CIRCLE	Advance and retire twice.	8 bars
B	HOUSE	All four couples dance house around.	8 bars
C	HOME	All four couples dance around at home	8 bars
D	FIGURE	(a) ADVANCE & RETIRE: TOP COUPLES advance to centre and retire once.	4 bars
		(b) CROSSOVER: The TOP LADIES dance across to each others places while the TOP GENTS dance in place (2 bars), then the TOP GENTS dance across to each others places while the TOP LADIES dance in place (2 bars).	4 bars
		(c) SWING: TOP COUPLES swing in place.	8 bars
		(d) ADVANCE & RETIRE: TOP COUPLES advance to centre and retire once.	4 bars
		(e) CROSSOVER: TOP COUPLES repeat (b) to bring them back to their own places again.	4 bars
		(f) SWING: TOP COUPLES swing in place.	8 bars
E	HOUSE	All four couples dance house around.	8 bars
F	HOME	All four couples dance around at home.	8 bars
G	FIGURE	SIDE COUPLES repeat D.	32 bars
H	HOUSE	All four couples dance house around.	8 bars
I	HOME	All four couples dance around at home.	8 bars

'Back To Back & Reel of Three'

3rd Figure

Reel - 152 bars

Opening Position: All dancers face to centre, joining hands in a circle.

A CIRCLE   Advance and retire twice.   8 bars

B FIGURE   (a) PASS THROUGH: TOP COUPLES advance and pass through, 1st tops on outside, and then retire and pass through, 1st tops on inside.

     1st tops seperate for last two bars. The lady turns clockwise and dances in beside 2nd sides gent, and the gent turns anti-clockwise and dances in beside 1st sides lady.

     2nd tops dance in place for last two bars.

     Each couple should take two bars to pass through, dance two bars while they change from the inside to the outside or vice versa, take two bars to pass back through, and two bars to dance in place or turn in beside the other couples.   8 bars

     (b) ADVANCE & RETIRE: The two groups of three dancers facing each other join hands and advance to the centre and retire twice.   8 bars

     (c) SWING: The two groups of three swing in place arms around each others backs.

     They should make sure to come out of the swing in time for the next movement.   8 bars
     (see page 85)

C CIRCLE   Reform the circle and advance and retire twice.   8 bars

D FIGURE   Repeat B. This time the 2ND TOPS dance forward on the outside, back on the inside and turn to make the threes with the side couples.   24 bars

E CIRCLE   Reform the circle and advance and retire twice.   8 bars

F FIGURE   SIDE COUPLES repeat B. 1st sides dance the figure.   24 bars

G CIRCLE   Reform the circle and advance and retire twice.   8 bars

H FIGURE   SIDE COUPLES repeat B. 2nd sides dance the figure.   24 bars

I CIRCLE   Reform the circle and advance and retire twice.   8 bars

J SWING   All four couples swing in place.   8 bars

'Change Places'

4th Figure   Polka - 104 bars

Opening Position: Couples adopt the standard position.

A	CHANGE PLACES	(a) <u>TOPS:</u> 1ST TOPS and 2ND TOPS dance half-way around the house to each others place while the side couples dance in place.	4 bars
		(b) <u>SIDES:</u> 1ST SIDES and 2ND SIDES dance half-way around the house to each others place while the top couples dance in place.	4 bars
		(c) <u>TOPS:</u> 1ST TOPS and 2ND TOPS dance half-way around the house back to their own places while the side couples dance in place.	4 bars
		(d) <u>SIDES:</u> 1ST SIDES and 2ND SIDES dance half-way around the house back to their own places while the top couples dance in place.	4 bars
B	<u>HOME</u>	TOP COUPLES dance around at home.	8 bars
C	<u>HOUSE</u>	TOP COUPLES dance house around.	8 bars
D	<u>HOME</u>	All four couples dance around at home.	8 bars
F	<u>HOUSE</u>	All four couples dance house around.	8 bars
F	CHANGE PLACES	Repeat A. On this occasion the side couples change first.	16 bars
G	<u>HOME</u>	SIDE COUPLES dance around at home.	8 bars
H	<u>HOUSE</u>	SIDE COUPLES dance house around.	8 bars
I	<u>HOME</u>	All four couples dance around at home.	8 bars
J	<u>HOUSE</u>	All four couples dance house around.	8 bars

363505

THE MONAGHAN SET

'Change All Around'

Hornpipe - 128 bars

Opening Position: All dancers face to centre, joining hands in a circle.
(see page 81)

A	CIRCLE	Advance and retire twice.	8 bars
B	HOUSE	All four couples dance house around.	8 bars
C	HOME & CHANGE	All four couples dance around at home. During the last two bars the gents, keeping their partners right hands in their left hands, turn their partners under their left arms so that when the circle forms again the gents have their original partners to their left, and they have new partners to their right.	8 bars
D	CIRCLE	Reform the circle and advance and retire twice.	8 bars
E	HOUSE	All four couples dance house around.	8 bars
F	HOME & CHANGE	Repeat C The ladies move one place around again.	8 bars
G	CIRCLE	Reform the circle and advance and retire twice.	8 bars
H	HOUSE	All four couples dance house around.	8 bars
I	HOME & CHANGE	Repeat C. The ladies move one place around again.	8 bars
J	CIRCLE	Reform the circle and advance and retire twice.	8 bars
K	HOUSE	All four couples dance house around.	8 bars
L	HOME & CHANGE	Repeat C. The ladies move one place around again to rejoin their original partners.	8 bars
M	CIRCLE	Reform the circle and advance and retire twice.	8 bars
N	HOUSE	All four couples dance house around.	8 bars
O	HOME	All four couples dance around at home, doubling the last two bars	8 bars

The Lancers

LEARNED IN CRUSHEEN, CO. CLARE IN
1983 FROM PATRICIA MULLINS AND HER
NEIGHBOURS.

THE DANCING OF THIS SET WAS REVIVED
BY THE PEOPLE OF CRUSHEEN AFTER A
LAPSE OF SOME YEARS, UNDER THE GUID-
ANCE OF LOCAL PEOPLE WHO DANCED IT
BEFORE IT LAPSED.

A LANCERS SET IS DANCED AROUND
KILKENNY, AND ALSO IN THE ROSCOMMON
AREA, ACCORDING TO REPORTS, AND IT
MAY ALSO BE DANCED IN OTHER AREAS.
I DO NOT KNOW HOW THEY COMPARE WITH
THE VERSION HERE, AS I HAVE NOT YET
SEEN THESE DANCES.

AS DANCED IN CRUSHEEN IT IS PER-
FORMED IN THE SAME STYLE AS THE
OTHER CLARE SETS, USING THE SAME
SLIDING STEP.

THE LANCERS

1st Figure   Reel - 160 bars

Opening Position: All four couples join hands in front and face anti-clockwise around the circle, gents on the inside. (see page 82)

A LEAD
  AROUND
All four couples dance anti-clockwise around until back in original places.

During the last two bars each couple changes to the standard position by the gent turning the lady clockwise under both arms.   8 bars

B SWING   All four couples swing in place.   8 bars

C FIGURE (a) ADVANCE & SWING: 1ST TOPS GENT & 2ND TOPS LADY dance to the centre, arriving left shoulder to left shoulder (2 bars), and then turn clockwise to face each other (2 bars). They then join up and swing in place (4 bars). (see page 83)   8 bars

       (b) SQUARE: 1ST TOPS & 2ND TOPS LADIES & GENTS dance around the sides of a square inside, the ladies going anti-clockwise and the gents clockwise, taking two bars to dance along each side of the square. (see page 83)

(Because 1st tops gent and 2nd tops lady are starting from the mid-point of one side of the square the steps they dance to the first two bars must be shortened.)   8 bars

       (c) SWING: At the end of (b) each dancer from the top couples goes to the nearest dancer from the side couples and swings with them.   8 bars

       (d) SWING: The four original couples re-form and all four couples swing in place.   8 bars

D FIGURE   Repeat C, the figure being danced by 2ND TOPS GENT & 1ST TOPS LADY.   32 bars

E FIGURE   Repeat C, the figure being danced by 1ST SIDES GENT & 2ND SIDES LADY.   32 bars

F FIGURE   Repeat C, the figure being danced by 2ND SIDES GENT & 1ST & 1ST SIDES LADY.   32 bars

G HOUSE   All four couples dance house around, doubling the last two bars.   8 bars

THE LANCERS

Opening Position: All four couples join hands in front and face anti-clockwise around the circle, gents on the inside.

A LEAD AROUND
All four couples dance anti-clockwise around until back in original places.

During the last two bars each couple changes to the standard position by the gent turning the lady clockwise under both arms.   **8 bars**

B SWING
All four couples swing in place.   **8 bars**

C FIGURE (a) **HOUSE:**   1ST TOPS dance around the house inside.   **8 bars**

    (b) **TURN THE LADY:** 1ST TOPS GENT turns his partner clockwise four times under his right arm, while dancing in place himself.   **8 bars**

    (c) **PASS BY:** 1ST TOPS LADY & GENT dance past each other to the sides and turn (gent dances towards side couple to his right, lady towards side couple to her left), (4 bars).

They then dance back to opposite sides and turn, top lady taking hand of side gent, and top gent taking hand of side lady (4 bars).

During the last two bars 2nd tops dance into place at the other end of the lines.   **8 bars**

    (d) **ADVANCE & RETIRE:** The two lines advance towards each other and retire, twice. The second time retiring the end couples (on this occasion the tops) do not retire but dance the two bars in place in the centre.   **8 bars**

    (e) **SWING:** All four couples swing in place.   **8 bars**

D FIGURE
Repeat C, the figure being danced by 2ND TOPS.   **40 bars**

E FIGURE
Repeat C, the figure being danced by 1ST SIDES.   **40 bars**

F FIGURE
Repeat C, the figure being danced by 2ND SIDES.   **40 bars**

G HOUSE
All four couples dance house around, doubling the last two bars.   **8 bars**

THE LANCERS

Opening Position: All four couples join hands in front and face anti-clockwise around the circle, gents on the inside.

A LEAD AROUND   All four couples dance anti-clockwise around until back in original places.

During the last two bars each couple changes to the standard position by the gent turning the lady clockwise under both arms.   8 bars

B SWING   All four couples swing in place.   8 bars

C FIGURE   (a) <u>LADIES IN:</u> The four ladies dance forwards to the centre and back out, twice. The second time dancing in they bow their heads.   8 bars

(b) <u>GENTS IN:</u> The four gents repeat (a).   8 bars

(c) <u>WHEEL:</u> The four gents link left hands in the centre and, with right arms around their partners waists, dance around anti-clockwise.   8 bars

(d) <u>WHEEL BACK:</u> The four couples reverse direction, (each dancer turns towards their partner to change direction), the four gents link right hands in the centre and, with left arms around their partners waists, dance in a clockwise direction back around to their original places.   8 bars

(e) <u>BIG CHRISTMAS:</u> All dancers link up together into a big circle, arms behind each other's backs and dance around clockwise (8 bars).

Then keeping the same position, they reverse direction and dance back around anti-clockwise to their original places, (8 bars).

When changing from the wheel position to the circle position at the beginning of this movement dancers must again turn towards their partners on their way into the circle.

When dancing clockwise around in the Big Christmas each dancer's right foot should come down on the beat of the music. When dancing anti-clockwise the left foot should come down. (see page 83)   16 bars

(f) <u>SWING:</u> All four couples swing in place.   8 bars

D FIGURE   Repeat C.   56 bars

E HOUSE   All four couples dance house around, doubling the last two bars.   8 bars

THE LANCERS

Opening Position: All four couples join hands in front and face anti-clockwise around the circle, gents on the inside.

A LEAD AROUND   All four couples dance anti-clockwise around until back in original places.

During the last two bars each couple changes to the standard position by the gent turning the lady clockwise under both arms.   8 bars

B SWING   All four couples swing in place.   8 bars

C FIGURE   (a) HOUSE: 1ST TOPS dance around the house inside.   8 bars

(b) LEAD AROUND: 1ST TOPS & 2ND TOPS lead around inside, dancing in a clockwise direction, ladies at the centre beside each other. (see page 83)   8 bars

(c) WHEEL: Each top couple regains original place, passes it, and gives right hands to the side couple to their left.

The two groups of four dancers, right hands joined, wheel clockwise (4 bars), then change direction, join left hands and wheel back anti-clockwise (4 bars).   8 bars

(d) LITTLE CHRISTMAS: Each group of dancers forms into a tight circle, arms around each other's backs, and dances around clockwise.

Each gent should have his right arm around his partner's back under her left arm so as to be able to move easily into the swing.

While dancing around in the Little Christmas each dancer's right foot should come down on the beat of the music.   8 bars

(e) SWING: The circles break into the original couples who swing in place.   8 bars

D FIGURE   Repeat C. 2ND TOPS dance around the house at (a).
In (b) the lead around is performed anti-clockwise, the gents at the centre beside each other.
In (c) the top couples join up with the side couples to their right.   40 bars

E FIGURE   Repeat C. 1ST SIDES dance around the house at (a).   40 bars

F FIGURE   Repeat C. 2ND SIDES dance around the house at (a).
In (b) the lead around is performed anti-clockwise, the gents at the centre beside each other.
In (c) the side couples join up with the top couples to their right.   40 bars

G HOUSE   All four couples dance house around, doubling the last two bars.   8 bars

THE LANCERS

5th Figure

Reel - 192 bars

Opening Position: All four couples join hands in front and face anti-clockwise around the circle, gents on the inside.

A LEAD
AROUND

All four couples dance anti-clockwise around until back in original places.

During the last two bars each couple changes to the standard position by the gent turning the lady clockwise under both arms. **8 bars**

B SWING

All four couples swing in place. **8 bars**

C FIGURE

(a) CHAIN & LINE UP: Starting with a right hand to their own partners ladies and gents chain around clockwise and anti-clockwise respectively. Half-way around partners meet each other and swing once. The chain is then continued to bring all dancers back to their original places. They do not form couples again, but line up as follows:

LINE UP: On the first occasion the line forms up behind 1st tops lady, facing out of the set in the direction of 1st tops position. As each couple gets into place in the line each lady should be in front of her partner. (see page 84)

The line forms in the following order: The leading couple, the couple to the left of the leading couple, the couple to the right of the leading couple, and the couple opposite the leading couple, with each lady in front of her partner. **16 bars**

(b) SIDE STEP: The line splits. Gents step sideways to the left and ladies sideways to the right, (4 bars). The lines then return in opposite directions, passing through each other to the opposite sides, and turn to face each other, (4 bars). (see page 84) **8 bars**

(c) ADVANCE & RETIRE: Lines join hands and advance and retire twice. **8 bars**

(d) DANCE TO PLACE & SWING: Each dancer dances back to their original place in four bars and then couples join up and swing in place for four bars. i.e. dancers at the end of the lines dance towards each other and meet in the centre. In the case of the other two couples the lady and gent that are in their correct places simply dance in place, and their partners dance across to them. (see page 84) **8 bars**

D FIGURE

Repeat C, the line forming behind 2ND TOPS. **40 bars**

E FIGURE

Repeat C, the line forming behind 1ST SIDES. **40 bars**

F FIGURE

Repeat C, the line forming behind 2ND SIDES. **40 bars**

G HOUSE

All four couples dance house around, doubling the last two bars. **8 bars**

18

The South Galway Reel Set

LEARNED IN DUBLIN FROM BENEN FAHY OF GALWAY,

THIS SET IS DANCED IN NORTH CLARE AND SOUTH GALWAY, TO MY KNOWLEDGE, AND POSSIBLY IN OTHER AREAS.

THE STEP USED IN GALWAY IS DIFFERENT FROM THE ONE EMPLOYED FOR DANCING THE VARIOUS CLARE SETS, AND PRODUCES A QUITE DIFFERENT VISUAL EFFECT. I HAVE TRIED TO EXPLAIN IT IN THE SECTION DEALING WITH STEPS BUT THIS ONE IN PARTICULAR NEEDS TO BE SEEN TO BE APPRECIATED.

THE SOUTH GALWAY REEL SET

1st Figure

Reel - 56 bars

Opening Position: Couples adopt the standard position.

A HOUSE   All four couples dance house around.   8 bars

B FIGURE   PASS THROUGH & RETURN: 1ST TOPS & 1ST SIDES turn
                towards each other, and 2ND TOPS & 2ND SIDES turn towards
                each other.

                All four couples dance forward and pass through, ladies on the
                inside passing left shoulder to left shoulder.

                After passing, each couple dances into the position just vacated
                by the couple with whom they are dancing, the lady passing in
                front of the gent, and they turn again to face each other.
                (4 bars)

                All couples now repeat this movement to bring them back to their
                original positions.   (4 bars)
                                                                              8 bars

C SWING   All four couples swing in place.
                                                                              8 bars

D HOUSE   All four couples dance house around.
                                                                              8 bars

E FIGURE   Repeat B.
                                                                              8 bars

F SWING   All four couples swing in place.
                                                                              8 bars

THE SOUTH GALWAY REEL SET

Opening Position: Couples adopt the standard position.

A	HOUSE	All four couples dance house around.	8 bars
B	FIGURE	(a) ADVANCE & RETIRE: 1ST TOPS & 1ST SIDES turn towards each other, and 2ND TOPS & 2ND SIDES turn towards each other. They advance and retire once.	4 bars
		(b) PASS THROUGH & TURN: The couples facing each other advance again and pass through, the ladies on the inside passing left shoulder to left shoulder, and then, the ladies passing in front of their partners, dance into the position of the couple with whom they are dancing, and turn to face each other again.	4 bars
		(c) ADVANCE & RETIRE: Repeat (a).	4 bars
		(d) PASS THROUGH & TURN: Repeat (b).	4 bars
C	SWING	All four couples swing in place.	8 bars
D	HOUSE	All four couples dance house around.	8 bars
E	FIGURE	Repeat B.	16 bars
F	SWING	All four couples swing in place.	8 bars

3rd Figure   Reel - 88 bars

Opening Position: Couples adopt the standard position.

A HOUSE   All four couples dance house around.   8 bars

B FIGURE (a) ADVANCE & RETIRE: All four couples advance to the centre
              and retire, once.   4 bars

          (b) CHANGE: All four couples dance half-way around the house to
              each other's position.   4 bars

          (c) ADVANCE & RETIRE: All four couples advance to the centre and
              retire, once.   4 bars

          (d) CHANGE: All four couples dance half-way around the house to
              return to their own positions again.   4 bars

          (e) HOUSE: All four couples dance house around.   8 bars

C SWING   All four couples swing in place.   8 bars

D HOUSE   All four couples dance house around.   8 bars

E FIGURE   Repeat B.   24 bars

F SWING   All four couples swing in place.   8 bars

THE SOUTH GALWAY REEL SET

4th Figure Jig - 88 bars

Opening Position: Couples adopt the standard position.

A HOUSE   All four couples dance house around.   8 bars

B FIGURE   (a) HOUSE: TOP COUPLES dance house around.   8 bars

        (b) ADVANCE & RETIRE: All four couples advance to centre and
retire, twice.   8 bars

        (c) HOUSE: All four couples dance house around.   8 bars

C SWING   All four couples swing in place.   8 bars

D HOUSE   All four couples dance house around.   8 bars

E FIGURE   Repeat B. [SIDE COUPLES dance house at (a)].   24 bars

F SWING   All four couples swing in place.   8 bars

5th Figure   Reel - 104 bars

Opening Position: Couples adopt the standard position.

A HOUSE   All four couples dance house around.   8 bars

B FIGURE   (a) ADVANCE & RETIRE: 1ST TOPS & 1ST SIDES turn towards each
                 other, and 2ND TOPS & 2ND SIDES turn towards each other.
                 They advance and retire once.   4 bars

            (b) LADIES CHANGE: The ladies in each pair of couples dance
                 across to each other's place.   4 bars

            (c) HOUSE: The four ladies pick up new partners and all four
                 couples dance house around.   8 bars

            (d) ADVANCE & RETIRE: Repeat (a).   4 bars

            (e) LADIES CHANGE: Repeat (b) to bring the ladies back to their
                 own partners.   4 bars

            (f) HOUSE: All four couples dance house around.   8 bars

C SWING   All four couples swing in place.   8 bars

D HOUSE   All four couples dance house around.   8 bars

E FIGURE   Repeat B.   32 bars

F CIRCLE   All dancers link up together into a big circle, arms behind each
               other's backs, and dance around clockwise.   8 bars

The Caledonian

LEARNED FROM A WRITTEN VERSION TAKEN DOWN BY UNA BEAN UI ROCHAIN FROM MARTY MALLEY, KNOCKLISCRANE, MILTOWN MALBAY.

THE CALEDONIAN IS THE MOST WIDELY DANCED SET IN COUNTY CLARE, WITH SEVERAL VERSIONS IN EXISTENCE THERE, AND A FEW IN OTHER PARTS OF THE COUNTRY. THE DIFFERENCES BETWEEN THEM CAN BE SLIGHT, BUT ENOUGH TO CAUSE CONFUSION SHOULD ONE ENTER A SET AND ATTEMPT TO DANCE A DIFFERENT VERSION FROM THE REST OF THE DANCERS. COMMON COURTESY, AS WELL AS COMMON SENSE WOULD SUGGEST THAT VISITORS ESTABLISH HOW A SET IS DANCED IN ANY LOCALITY BEFORE PARTICIPATING THEM-SELVES.

THE CALEDONIAN

1st Figure   Reel - 128 bars

Opening Position: All face to centre, joining hands in a circle.

A START   (a) CIRCLE: Advance and retire twice.   8 bars

           (b) HOME: All four couples dance around at home.   8 bars

B FIGURE   (a) SLIDE & CHANGE: TOP COUPLES advance to centre and retire
               once (4 bars), and then dance half-way around the house to each
               other's places, (4 bars). This movement is then repeated to bring
               them back to their own positions again.   16 bars

           (b) HOME: TOP COUPLES dance around at home.   8 bars

           (c) SLIDE & CHANGE: TOP COUPLES repeat (a).   16 bars

C MIDDLE   (a) SLIDE: All four couples advance to centre and retire once.   4 bars

           (b) HOME: SIDE COUPLES dance around at home.   4 bars

D FIGURE   SIDE COUPLES repeat B.   40 bars

E FINISH   (a) SLIDE: All four couples advance to centre and retire once.   4 bars

           (b) HOME: All four couples dance around at home.   4 bars

           (c) HOUSE: All four couples dance house around.   8 bars

THE CALEDONIAN

2nd Figure   Reel - 96 bars

Opening Position: All dancers face to centre, joining hands in a circle.

A START   (a) CIRCLE: Advance and retire twice.   8 bars

           (b) HOME: All four couples dance around at home.   8 bars

B FIGURE   (a) HOUSE: TOP COUPLES dance around the house inside.   8 bars

           (b) HOME: TOP COUPLES dance around at home.   8 bars

           (c) HOUSE: TOP COUPLES dance around the house inside.   8 bars

C MIDDLE   (a) SLIDE: All four couples advance to centre and retire once.   4 bars

           (b) HOME: SIDE COUPLES dance around at home.   4 bars

D FIGURE   SIDE COUPLES repeat B.   24 bars

E FINISH   (a) SLIDE: All four couples advance to centre and retire once.   4 bars

           (b) HOME: All four couples dance around at home.   4 bars

           (c) HOUSE: All four couples dance house around.   8 bars

THE CALEDONIAN

3rd Figure   Reel - 192 bars

Opening Position: All dancers face to centre, joining hands in a circle.

A START   (a) CIRCLE: Advance and retire twice.   8 bars

           (b) HOME: All four couples dance around at home.   8 bars

B FIGURE   (a) SLIDE & HOME: TOP COUPLES advance to centre and retire once (4 bars), and then dance around at home (4 bars).   8 bars

           (b) SLIDE & CHANGE: TOP COUPLES advance to centre and retire once (4 bars), and then dance half-way around the house to each other's place, (4 bars).   8 bars

           (c) SLIDE & HOME: TOP COUPLES repeat (a).   8 bars

           (d) SLIDE & CHANGE: TOP COUPLES repeat (b) to bring them back to their original positions.   8 bars

           (e) HOME: TOP COUPLES dance around at home.   8 bars

           (f) SLIDE & HOME: TOP COUPLES repeat (a)   8 bars

           (g) SLIDE & CHANGE: TOP COUPLES repeat (b).   8 bars

           (h) SLIDE & HOME: TOP COUPLES repeat (c).   8 bars

           (i) SLIDE & CHANGE: TOP COUPLES repeat (d).   8 bars

C MIDDLE   (a) SLIDE: All four couples advance to centre and retire once.   4 bars

           (b) HOME: SIDE COUPLES dance around at home.   4 bars

D FIGURE   SIDE COUPLES repeat B.   72 bars

E FINISH   (a) SLIDE: All four couples advance to centre and retire once.   4 bars

           (b) HOME: All four couples dance at home.   4 bars

           (c) HOUSE: All four couples dance house around.   8 bars

THE CALEDONIAN

Jig - 160 bars

Opening Position: All dancers face to centre, joining hands in a circle.

A **START**   (a) <u>CIRCLE:</u> Advance and retire twice.   8 bars

    (b) <u>HOME:</u> All four couples dance around at home.   8 bars

B **FIGURE**   (a) <u>HOUSE & HOME:</u> TOP COUPLES dance around the house inside (8 bars), and then dance around at home, (8 bars)   16 bars

    (b) <u>SLIDE & CHANGE PARTNERS:</u> TOP COUPLES advance and retire once (4 bars), then the couples **separate** and while the ladies dance on the spot, the gents dance in an anti-clockwise direction over to join up with the opposite ladies, (4 bars).   8 bars

    (c) <u>HOUSE & HOME:</u> TOP COUPLES (top ladies from their own positions, with their new partners) dance around the house inside (8 bars), and then dance around at home (8 bars).   16 bars

    (d) <u>SLIDE & CHANGE PARTNERS:</u> TOP COUPLES repeat B to bring the gents back to their original partners again.   8 bars

    (e) <u>HOUSE:</u> TOP COUPLES dance around the house inside.   8 bars

C **MIDDLE**   (a) <u>SLIDE:</u> All four couples advance to centre and retire once.   4 bars

    (b) <u>HOME:</u> SIDE COUPLES dance around at home.   4 bars

D **FIGURE**   SIDE COUPLES repeat B.   56 bars

E **FINISH**   (a) <u>SLIDE:</u> All four couples advance to centre and retire once.   4 bars

    (b) <u>HOME:</u> All four couples dance around at home.   4 bars

    (c) <u>HOUSE:</u> All four couples dance house around.   8 bars

THE CALEDONIAN

5th Figure   Reel - 256 bars

Opening Position: All dancers face to centre, joining hands in a circle.

A   START   (a) CIRCLE: Advance and retire twice.   8 bars

              (b) HOME: All four couples dance around at home.   8 bars

B   FIGURE   (a) HOUSE & HOME: TOP COUPLES dance around the house inside
                  (8 bars), and then dance around at home, (8 bars). 16 bars

              (b) SLIDE & CHANGE PARTNERS: TOP COUPLES advance and
                  retire once (4 bars); then the couples separate and the gents
                  dance in an anti-clockwise direction around each other to pick up
                  the side ladies to their left (4 bars). The side ladies dance on
                  the spot for the last 4 bars.   8 bars

              (c) HOUSE & HOME: TOP GENTS and their new partners dance
                  around the house inside (8 bars), starting and finishing at their
                  new partners position, and then dance around at home, (8 bars). 16 bars

              (d) SLIDE & CHANGE PARTNERS: TOP GENTS and their new part-
                  ners repeat (b). The gents move one place around again to pick
                  up the opposite top ladies.   8 bars

              (e) HOUSE & HOME: TOP GENTS and their new partners repeat (c) 16 bars

              (f) SLIDE & CHANGE PARTNERS: TOP GENTS and their new part-
                  ners repeat (b). The gents move one place around again to pick
                  up the side ladies.   8 bars

              (g) HOUSE & HOME: TOP GENTS and their new partners repeat (c) 16 bars

              (h) SLIDE & CHANGE PARTNERS: TOP GENTS and their new part-
                  ners repeat (b). The gents move one place around again to pick
                  up their original partners.   8 bars

              (i) HOUSE: TOP COUPLES dance around the house inside.   8 bars

C   MIDDLE   (a) SLIDE: All four couples advance to centre and retire once. 4 bars

              (b) HOME: SIDE COUPLES dance around at home   4 bars

D   FIGURE   SIDE COUPLES repeat B   104 bars

E   FINISH   (a) SLIDE: All four couples advance to centre and retire once 4 bars

              (b) HOME: All four couples dance around at home.   4 bars

              (c) HOUSE: All four couples dance house around   8 bars

THE CALEDONIAN

Hornpipe - 40 bars

Opening Position: Couples adopt the standard position.

A BODY   Each couple advances to the centre and retires back to their starting
           place (2 bars), then dances around to the position of the couple on
           their right (2 bars).

           This movement is repeated three more times (12 bars), the couples
           ending up back in their original positions.   16 bars

B SLIDE   All four couples advance to the centre and retire once.   4 bars

C HOME   All four couples dance around at home.   4 bars

D HOUSE   All four couples dance house around.   8 bars

The Mazurka Set

LEARNED IN ENNIS IN 1983 FROM SEAN McMAHON AND MAIRTIN BYRNES. THIS SET IS DANCED IN CLARE AND GALWAY AND IS ANOTHER SET WHERE VARIATIONS CAN OCCUR DEPENDING UPON WHERE IT IS DANCED.

LIKE THE PLAIN, THE CALEDONIAN AND THE LANCERS, THE KIND OF STEP USED FOR REEL FIGURES THROUGHOUT CLARE SHOULD BE USED WHEN DANCING THIS SET.

I WAS HESITANT ABOUT CALLING IT THE 'MAZURKA' SET, AS IT SEEMS TO BE UNIVERSALLY REFERRED TO AS 'THE MASSERKS'. I HAVE DONE SO ON THE ASSUMPTION THAT THE LATTER TITLE IS A LOCAL DERIVATION FROM 'MAZURKA'.

THE MAZURKA SET

'Little Christmas'

1st Figure   Reel - 144 bars

Opening Position: All dancers face to centre, joining hands in a circle.

A <u>CIRCLE</u>   Advance and retire twice.   8 bars

B <u>FIGURE</u>   (a) <u>SWING:</u> All four couples swing in place.   8 bars

          (b) <u>HOUSE:</u> 1ST TOPS dance around the house inside,   8 bars

          (c) <u>LITTLE CHRISTMAS:</u>   Couple who have danced house turn to couple on their left, and form a tight circle with them, arms behind each other's backs. They dance in a circle clockwise, and the other two couples do likewise.   8 bars

          (d) <u>HOUSE:</u> All four couples dance house around.   8 bars

C <u>FIGURE</u>   Repeat B. [1ST SIDES dance house at (b)].   32 bars

D <u>FIGURE</u>   Repeat B. [2ND TOPS dance house at (b)].   32 bars

E <u>FIGURE</u>   Repeat B. [2ND SIDES dance house at (b)].   32 bars

          Last two bars of final house around should be doubled.
          i.e. Ladies instead of dancing: R L R - L R L - R
                         dance: R L - R - L - R

          Gents, instead of dancing: L R L - R L R - L
                     dance: L - R - L - R - L

'Advance & Retire'

2nd Figure   Reel - 144 bars

Opening Position: All dancers face to centre, joining hands in a circle.

A CIRCLE   Advance and retire twice.   8 bars

B FIGURE   (a) SWING: All four couples swing in place.   8 bars

           (b) HOUSE: 1ST TOPS dance around the house inside.   8 bars

           (c) ADVANCE & RETIRE: The couples who have danced house face
               the couple to their left. These two couples advance towards each
               other and retire, twice. The other two couples do likewise.   8 bars

           (d) HOUSE: All four couples dance house around.   8 bars

C FIGURE   Repeat B [1ST SIDES dance house at (b)].   32 bars

D FIGURE   Repeat B. [2ND TOPS dance house . (b)].   32 bars

E FIGURE   Repeat B. [2ND SIDES dance house at (b)].   32 bars

               Last two bars of final house around should be doubled, as in first
               figure.

THE MAZURKA SET

'High Gates'

3rd Figure   Reel - 144 bars

Opening Position: All dancers face to centre, joining hands in a circle.

A CIRCLE   Advance and retire twice.   8 bars

B FIGURE   (a) SWING: All four couples swing in place.   8 bars

            (b) HOUSE: 1ST TOPS dance around the house inside.   8 bars

            (c) HIGH GATES: The gent of the couple who have danced house
                raises his partners right hand with his left hand and reaches under
                the raised arms with his right hand to take the right hand of the
                lady from the couple to their left and bring her through. (She
                keeps dancing around 1st tops couple anti-clockwise until it is her
                turn to pass through again.)

                Then 1st tops lady passes under her partner's right arm, followed
                by her partner. Dancing around, 1st tops lady again passes under
                her partner's right arm, followed by her partner. Finally the lady
                from the other couple, still holding the hand of the 1st tops gent,
                passes under the gent's left, and lady's right arms of 1st tops
                couple.

                Having danced completely around 1st tops she should pass through
                this time in the opposite direction to the first time, heading back
                towards her partner. (see page 85)   8 bars

            (d) HOUSE: All four couples dance house around.   8 bars

C FIGURE   Repeat B. [1ST SIDES dance house at (b)].   32 bars

D FIGURE   Repeat B. [2ND TOPS dance house at (b)].   32 bars

E FIGURE   Repeat B. [2ND SIDES dance house at (b)].   32 bars

                Last two bars of final house around should be doubled, as in first
                figure.

35

THE MAZURKA SET

'Swing'

Reel - 128 bars

Opening Position: All dancers face to centre, joining hands in a circle.

A CIRCLE   Advance and retire twice.   8 bars

B FIGURE   (a) SWING: All four couples swing in place.   8 bars

(b) HOUSE: 1ST TOPS and 2ND TOPS dance around the house inside.   8 bars

(c) SWING: 1ST & 2ND TOPS GENTS swing with all four ladies in turn, starting with the ladies to their left. All four couples swing for last 8 bars.   32 bars

(d) HOUSE: All four couples dance house around.   8 bars

C FIGURE   Repeat B. [SIDE COUPLES & SIDE GENTS dance the movements at (b) and (c)].   56 bars

Last two bars of final house around should be doubled, as in first figure.

THE MAZURKA SET

'Chain'

5th Figure   Reel - 176 bars

Opening Position: All dancers face to centre, joining hands in a circle.

A CIRCLE   Advance and retire twice.   8 bars

B FIGURE (a) SWING: All four couples swing in place.   8 bars

          (b) HOUSE: 1ST TOPS dance around the house inside.   8 bars

          (c) CHAIN: Ladies dancing clockwise, and gents anti clockwise, all
              dancers chain around, starting at their own partners with right
              hands, until they reach their own places again and swing in place
              to finish.   16 bars

          (d) HOUSE: All four couples dance house around.   8 bars

C FIGURE   Repeat B. [1ST SIDES dance house at (b)].   40 bars

D FIGURE   Repeat B. [2ND TOPS dance house at (b)].   40 bars

F FIGURE   Repeat B. [2ND SIDES dance house at (b)].   40 bars

              Last two bars of final house around should be doubled, as in first
              figure.

THE MAZURKA SET

'Face The Wall'

Reel - 208 bars

Opening Position: All dancers face to centre, joining hands in a circle.

A	CIRCLE	Advance and retire twice.	8 bars

B FIGURE (a) SWING: All four couples swing in place. **8 bars**

(b) HOUSE & LINE-UP: 1ST TOPS and the couple to their left (1ST SIDES) dance house around each other and end up facing out of the set in 1st tops direction, 1st tops first and 1st sides behind them. (8 bars)

The other two couples repeat this movement and end up lined up behind the first two couples. (8 bars) (see page 84)   **16 bars**

Starting from the couple in whose direction the line is facing, the other three couples should always be lined up behind them in the order that they come as you go clockwise around the set from that couple, gents on the left,· ladies on the right.

(c) ARCH: Gents circle off to the left, and ladies to the right, making a tight circle. They pass through their starting positions once and go around again. When the leading couple come around to the starting position the second time they face each other and form an arch with their arms. (8 bars) (see page 84)

The other couples, as they reach the arch, adopt the normal hold and dance under it and around anti-cloclwise to their own positions. (8 bars)   **16 bars**

(d) HOUSE: All four couples dance house around.   **8 bars**

C FIGURE   Repeat B. [1ST SIDES & 2ND TOPS dance house at (b)].   **48 bars**
Line faces out of set in direction of 1st sides.

D FIGURE   Repeat B.   [2nd TOPS & 2nd SIDES dance house at (b)].   **48 bars**
Line faces out of set in direction of 2nd tops.

E FIGURE   Repeat B. [2ND SIDES & 1ST TOPS dance house at (b)].   **48 bars**
Line faces out of set in direction of 2nd sides.

Last two bars of final house around should be doubled, as in first figure.

The Plain Set

LEARNED IN DUBLIN FROM CONNIE RYAN OF CO. TIPPERARY.

THIS SET IS REGARDED AS BEING A CLARE SET, ALTHOUGH IT SEEMS TO BE DANCED THERE LESS OFTEN THAN THE CALEDONIAN. IT IS CONSIDERED BY MANY, INCLUDING MYSELF, AS ONE OF THE MOST ENJOYABLE OF THE SETS TO DANCE.

BEING A CLARE SET, THE STEP COMMONLY DANCED TO REELS IN THAT COUNTY SHOULD BE EMPLOYED IN DANCING IT.

THE PLAIN SET

1st Figure Reel - 112 bars

Opening Position: All four couples join hands in front and face anti-clockwise around the circle, gents on the inside.

A LEAD AROUND All four couples dance anti-clockwise around until back in original places. During last bar each gent, without releasing hands, turns his partner clockwise under both arms and then adopts the standard hold. 8 bars

B HOME All four couples dance around at home. 8 bars

C FIGURE (a) PASS THROUGH: TOP COUPLES advance towards each other and pass through, ladies at the centre passing left shoulder to left shoulder.

After passing each couple joins right hands, each lady dances under the gent's right arm and the lady and gent dance around each other into place facing into the centre. 4 bars

(b) PASS THROUGH: TOP COUPLES repeat (a) to bring them back to their original places again. 4 bars

(c) HOME: TOP COUPLES dance around at home. 8 bars

(d) LADIES CHAIN: TOP LADIES dance to centre, chain with right hands and pass each other, give left hands to opposite gents, turn clockwise under their left arms and dance around behind them, the gents turning with the ladies.

The ladies then dance straight back to their own partners, join right hands with them, and turn clockwise and join left hands for the "lead around" position. 8 bars

(e) LEAD AROUND: 1st TOPS & 2nd TOPS lead around inside. They dance anti-clockwise half way around to reach each other's places and then face into the centre. 4 bars

(f) PASS THROUGH: TOP COUPLES repeat (a) to bring them back to their original places again. 4 bars

D HOME All four couples dance around at home. 8 bars

E FIGURE SIDE COUPLES repeat C. 32 bars

F HOME All four couples dance around at home. 8 bars

G HOUSE All four couples dance house around. 8 bars

40

THE PLAIN SET

2nd Figure

Reel - 128 bars

Opening Position: All four couples join hands in front and face anti-clockwise around the circle, gents on the inside.

A LEAD AROUND All four couples dance anti-clockwise around until back in original places. During last bar each gent, without releasing hands, turns his partner clockwise under both arms and then adopts the standard hold. 8 bars

B HOME All four couples dance around at home. 8 bars

C FIGURE (a) SLIDE: TOP COUPLES advance to centre and retire, once, with right hands joined. 4 bars

(b) CHANGE: TOP COUPLES dance around to each other's place. Each lady turns twice clockwise under the gents right arms as they dance around. The lady should dance ahead of the gent. 4 bars

(c) SLIDE: TOP COUPLES advance to centre and retire, once, with right hands joined. 4 bars

(d) CHANGE: TOP COUPLES repeat (b) to return to their own places again. 4 bars

(e) HOME: TOP COUPLES dance around at home. 8 bars

(f) SLIDE: TOP COUPLES repeat (a). 4 bars

(g) CHANGE: TOP COUPLES repeat (b). 4 bars

(h) SLIDE: TOP COUPLES repeat (c). 4 bars

(i) CHANGE: TOP COUPLES repeat (d). 4 bars

D HOME All four couples dance around at home. 8 bars

E FIGURE SIDE COUPLES repeat C. 40 bars

F HOME All four couples dance around at home. 8 bars

G HOUSE All four couples dance house around. 8 bars

41

THE PLAIN SET

3rd Figure

Reel - 176 bars

Opening Position: All four couples join hands in front and face anti-clockwise around the circle, gents on the inside.

A LEAD AROUND — All four couples dance anti-clockwise around until back in original places. During last bar each gent, without releasing hands, turns his partner clockwise under both arms and then adopts the standard hold.   8 bars

B HOME — All four couples dance around at home.   8 bars

C FIGURE
(a) LADIES CROSS & HOME: TOP LADIES dance straight across to the opposite gents (2 bars), and dance at home with them (6 bars).   8 bars

(b) GENTS CROSS & TURN: TOP GENTS dance straight across to their own partners (2 bars), join right hands with them and turn the ladies anti-clockwise under-arm, dancing in on the "wrong" (right-hand) side of their partners (2 bars).

Tops then join left hands and each dancer dances past his or her partner into the correct place, the lady turning clockwise under her partner's arm as she dances (2 bars). Then, dancing on the spot, the top ladies turn clockwise once more under their partners left arm and each top couple faces into the centre, joining hands in front (2 bars).   8 bars

(c) ADVANCE & RETIRE: TOP COUPLES, right hands joined, advance to the centre and retire, twice.   8 bars

(d) SLIDE & CHANGE: TOP COUPLES change to standard hold, advance to centre and retire once (4 bars), and then dance half-way around the house to their original positions (4 bars).   8 bars

(e) GENTS CROSS & HOME: Repeat (a).   8 bars

(f) LADIES CROSS & TURN: Repeat (b).   8 bars

(g) ADVANCE & RETIRE: Repeat (c).   8 bars

(h) SLIDE & CHANGE: Repeat (d).   8 bars

D HOME — All four couples dance around at home.   8 bars

E FIGURE — SIDE COUPLES repeat C.   64 bars

F HOME — All four couples dance around at home.   8 bars

G HOUSE — All four couples dance house around.   8 bars

42

THE PLAIN SET

4th Figure   **Reel - 256 bars**

Opening Position: All four couples join hands in front and face anti-clockwise around the circle, gents on the inside.

A LEAD AROUND — All four couples dance anti-clockwise around until back in original places. During last bar each gent, without releasing hands, turns his partner clockwise under both arms and adopts the standard hold.   8 bars

B HOME — All four couples dance around at home,   8 bars

C FIGURE
(a) LADIES CHAIN: TOP LADIES dance to the centre, chain with right hands and pass each other, give left hands to opposite gents and dance around behind them turning clockwise under the gents left arm, the gents turning with the ladies. After dancing around the opposite gents they dance straight across back to their own partners.   8 bars

(b) HOME: TOP COUPLES dance around at home.   8 bars

(c) HOUSE: 1ST TOPS dance around the house inside so as to reach the position of the opposite couple at the end of the eight bars, 1st tops lady dancing in on the left side of the opposite gent and facing in, and 1st tops gent facing the opposite gent. They then link up in the following way.
1st tops gent takes his own partner's right hand in his right hand and the opposite lady's left hand in his left hand. The opposite gent holds the ladies' other hands above the hands held by 1st tops gent. (see page 86)   8 bars

(d) ADVANCE & RETIRE: 1ST tops gent retires and the three dancers facing him advance to the centre (2 bars), return to the second tops position (2 bars) and come back to the centre again (2 bars). Then the 1st tops gent pulls the two ladies towards him. They each turn outwards from the gent between them, under the arms held by him, and then under the arms held by the 1st tops gent to come in on each side of him, with the opposite gent now alone facing the three, (2 bars). This whole movement is now repeated in the opposite direction, the group of three advancing (2 bars), retiring (2 bars) and advancing again (2 bars), the opposite gent dancing accordingly, and then the ladies are drawn out into a position between the two gents (2 bars).   16 bars

(e) LITTLE CHRISTMAS: 1ST TOPS & 2ND TOPS form into a tight circle, arms around each other's backs and dance around clockwise.   8 bars

(f) LADIES CHAIN: When the circle breaks gents retire to their places and ladies immediately repeat (a).   8 bars

(g) REPEAT: Repeat (b) to (f), 2ND TOPS dancing the figure.   48 bars

D HOME — All four couples dance around at home.   8 bars

E FIGURE — SIDE COUPLES repeat C.   104 bars

F HOME — All four couples dance around at home.   8 bars

G HOUSE — All four couples dance house around.   8 bars

THE PLAIN SET

Opening Position: All four couples join hands in front and face anti-clockwise around the circle, gents on the inside.

A LEAD AROUND — All four couples dance anti-clockwise around until back in original places. During last bar each gent, without releasing hands, turns his partner clockwise under both arms, and then adopts the standard hold.   8 bars

B SWING — All four couples swing in place.   8 bars

C HOUSE — All four couples dance house around.   8 bars

D FIGURE — (a) GALLOP: TOP COUPLES cross straight over to each other's place without turning, gents on the inside (2 bars). SIDE COUPLES do likewise (2 bars). TOP COUPLES cross back to their original places, ladies on the inside (2 bars). SIDE COUPLES do likewise (2 bars).   8 bars

(b) LADIES CHAIN: TOP LADIES chain with right hands in the centre and dance over to opposite gents. They are followed immediately by SIDE LADIES. (2 bars). Each lady gives left hand to opposite gent, turns clockwise under his left arm and dances around behind him, the gent turning with the lady. Each lady then dances to the left across in front of her opposite gent, giving right hands to the gent in the position one place to the right of their starting positions. They join right hands with this gent and dance anti-clockwise under the gents right arm into place. (see page 86)   8 bars

E SWING — All four couples swing in place.   8 bars

F HOUSE — All four couples dance house around.   8 bars

G FIGURE — Repeat D. The original top ladies are always first to cross in (a) and in (b).   16 bars

H SWING — All four couples swing in place.   8 bars

I HOUSE — All four couples dance house around.   8 bars

J FIGURE — Repeat D. Thr original top ladies are always first to cross in (a) and in (b).   16 bars

K SWING — All four couples swing in place.   8 bars

L HOUSE — All four couples dance house around.   8 bars

M FIGURE — Repeat D to bring the ladies back to their original partners again. The top ladies are always first to cross in (a) and in (b).   16 bars

N SWING — All four couples swing in place.   8 bars

O HOUSE — All four couples dance house around.   8 bars

THE PLAIN SET

6th Figure   Reel - 192 bars

Opening Position: All four couples join hands in front and face anti-clockwise around the circle, gents on the inside.

A LEAD   All four couples dance anti-clockwise around until back in original
   AROUND   places.   During the last bar each gent, without releasing hands, turns
             his partner clockwise under both arms and then adopts the standard
             hold.   8 bars

B HOME   All four couples dance around at home.   8 bars

C HOUSE   All four couples dance house around.   8 bars

D FIGURE   (a) HOME: All four couples dance around at home.   8 bars

             (b) LADIES IN: The four ladies advance to the centre and retire,
                  twice.   8 bars

             (c) GENTS WHEEL & CHANGE PARTNERS: The four gents join
                  right hand in the centre and dance around clockwise (4 bars).
                  then turn, join left hands in the centre and dance around anti-
                  clockwise (4 bars).
                  At the same time each lady dances around to the next position to
                  her right.   8 bars

             (d) HOME: The ladies join up with new partners and all four couples
                  dance around at home.   8 bars

E HOUSE   All four couples dance house around.   8 bars

F FIGURE   Repeat D.   At (c) the gents join left hands first.   32 bars

G HOUSE   All four couples dance house around.   8 bars

H FIGURE   Repeat D.   32 bars

I HOUSE   All four couples dance house around.   8 bars

J FIGURE   Repeat D.   At (c) the gents join left hands first.   32 bars

K HOUSE   All four couples dance house around.   8 bars

The Castle Set

LEARNED IN DUBLIN FROM CONNIE RYAN OF TIPPERARY AND BETTY McCOY OF DUBLIN.

THE CASTLE SET

Opening Position: Couples adopt the standard position.

A	HOUSE	TOP COUPLES dance around the house inside.	8 bars
B	PASS THROUGH	1st TOPS & 2ND TOPS advance towards each other and pass through, ladies in the centre, left shoulder to left shoulder (4 bars). When they reach the opposite side each dancer turns clockwise on the spot. The two couples advance and pass back through to their own places, ladies in the centre, right shoulder to right shoulder, and turn clockwise to face in again, (4 bars).	8 bars
C	ADVANCE & RETIRE	TOP COUPLES join right hands in front. They advance to the centre and retire twice.	8 bars
D	SWING	All four LADIES turn to the gents on their right and swing with them. At the end of the swing the ladies should end up to the right of their new partners.	8 bars
E	ADVANCE & RETIRE	All dancers join hands in a circle and advance to the centre and retire twice.	8 bars
F	SWING	The ladies return to their original partners and all four couples swing in place.	8 bars
G	REPEAT	TOP COUPLES repeat A to F.	48 bars
H	REPEAT	SIDE COUPLES repeat A to F. When sides dance the figure the ladies go to the gents on their left at D.	48 bars
I	REPEAT	SIDE COUPLES repeat A to F. The ladies go to the gents on their left at D.	48 bars

2nd Figure

Opening Position: Couples adopt the standard position.

A HOUSE TOP COUPLES dance around the house inside. 8 bars

B ADVANCE TOP COUPLES join right hands in front. They advance to the
& RETIRE centre and retire once. 4 bars

C CHANGE TOP LADIES dance straight across to the opposite gents (2 bars) and swing once with him (2 bars). 4 bars

D WHEEL TOP GENTS keep their hold on their new partners with their right arms and release their partners right hands. TOP LADIES join right hands in the centre and the top couples form a straight line, each couple facing clockwise around the circle. They wheel around in a clockwise direction until back in gents place. (see page 86) 8 bars

E SWING TOP COUPLES swing in place, (gents in their own place and ladies in the opposite places). 8 bars

F REPEAT TOP COUPLES repeat A to E.

During the repeat the top ladies return to their original partners. 32 bars

G REPEAT SIDE COUPLES repeat A to E.

During their first time through the figure the side ladies change partners. 32 bars

H REPEAT SIDE COUPLES repeat A to E.

During the repeat the side ladies return to their original partners. 32 bars

THE CASTLE SET

3rd Figure   Polka - 200 bars

Opening Position: Couples adopt the standard position.

A HOUSE   TOP COUPLES dance around the house inside.   8 bars

B LADIES   TOP LADIES dance to centre, chain with right hands and pass
  CHAIN   each other, give left hands to opposite gents and dance around
                 them, the gents turning with the ladies, chain with each other
                 again with right hands in the middle and give left hands to their
                 own partners and dance around them.   8 bars

C SWING   1ST TOPS GENT & 2ND TOPS LADY come out of chain to face
                 each other in the centre, each with their back to the couple on
                 their right.
                 They swing in the centre. At the end of the swing they seperate
                 and dance back between the side couples they had their backs to.
                 Each group of three dancers links arms behind each others backs.   8 bars
                 (see page 86)

D ADVANCE   1ST TOPS LADY & 2ND TOPS GENT advance to centre and retire
  & RETIRE   twice.   While they are advancing and retiring the SIDE THREES
                 dance in place.   8 bars

                 Then the SIDE THREES advance to the centre and retire, twice,
                 while the tops dance in place.   8 bars

E SWING   The four original couples re-form and swing in place. The dancers
                 should take two bars to dance into place and then join up and
                 swing.   8 bars

F REPEAT   TOP COUPLES repeat A to E.
                 1st tops lady and 2nd tops gent dance the figure at C, leading
                 into the swing from the same direction as their partners did, and
                 dancing in threes with the same couples as their partners.   48 bars

G REPEAT   SIDE COUPLES repeat A to E.
                 1st sides gent and 2nd sides lady dance the figure at C.   48 bars

H REPEAT   SIDE COUPLES repeat A to E.
                 1st sides lady and 2nd sides gent dance the figure at C.   48 bars

THE CASTLE SET

Opening Position: Couples adopt the standard position.

A HOUSE   1ST TOPS & 2ND TOPS dance around to each other's place in two bars, using the normal hornpipe step, (hop 1 2 3 - hop 1 2 3), and then dance on around, back to their own places in two bars, using the doubled hornpipe step (hop 1 hop 2 hop 3 hop 4).   4 bars

B CHANGE   TOP GENTS dance straight across to the opposite ladies, in two bars.   2 bars

C CLAP & STAMP   TOPS clap hands three times (1 bar) and dance on the spot (1 bar).   2 bars

D HOUSE   TOP GENTS with their new partners repeat A.   4 bars

E CHANGE   TOP GENTS dance straight across back to their own partners, in two bars.   2 bars

F CLAP & STAMP   TOP COUPLES repeat C.   2 bars

G REPEAT   TOP COUPLES repeat A to F.   16 bars

H HOUSE   TOP COUPLES repeat A.   4 bars

I REPEAT   SIDE COUPLES repeat A to H.   36 bars

J REPEAT   TOP COUPLES repeat A to H.   36 bars

K REPEAT   SIDE COUPLES repeat A to H.   36 bars

THE CASTLE SET

Opening Position: All dancers face to centre joining hands in a circle.

A	CIRCLE	Advance and retire twice.	8 bars

B HOUSE   TOP COUPLES dance around the house inside.   8 bars

C SLIDE &   (a) SLIDE: TOP COUPLES dance sideways to the centre. Gents
   CHANGE   dance: L-R-LRL, and ladies: R-L-RLR (2 bars). They then dance
                 back to their original places using the opposite steps, (2 bars).   4 bars

           (b) CHANGE: TOP COUPLES dance half-way around the house to
               each other's places.   4 bars

           (c) REPEAT: TOP COUPLES repeat (a) and (b) to bring them back
               to their original places again.   8 bars

D HOUSE   TOP COUPLES dance around the house inside.   8 bars

E LADIES   TOP LADIES dance to centre, chain with right elbows and pass
   CHAIN   each other, give left hands to opposite gents and dance around
             them, the gents turning with the ladies, dance to the centre again,
             chain with right hands and pass each other and join left hands
             with their partners left hands and dance around them, ending up
             on the outside of the circle facing anti-clockwise around, holding
             their partners left hands in front and right hands behind.

             During the last two bars the other two couples dance into the
             same position.   8 bars

F LEAD   All four couples dance around anti-clockwise to the next position
   AROUND   (2 bars) and dance in place (2 bars). This movement is repeated
             three more times until all couples are back in their original
             positions.   16 bars

G REPEAT   Repeat B to F, the figure being danced by the SIDE COUPLES.   56 bars

H REPEAT   Repeat B to F, the figure being danced by the TOP COUPLES.   56 bars

I REPEAT   Repeat B to F, the figure being danced by the SIDE COUPLES.   56 bars

J CIRCLE   Advance and retire twice.   8 bars

6th Figure   Slide - 120 bars

Opening Position: All dancers face to centre, joining hands in a circle.

A CIRCLE   Advance and retire twice.   8 bars

B SWING   All four couples swing in place.   8 bars

C CHANGE   All couples seperate.
  PARTNERS   Gents dance one bar into the centre and then dance one bar on
                the spot while turning clockwise to face around the set in an anti-
                clockwise direction.   During the same two bars the ladies dance
                around anti-clockwise to the next position to their right, level
                with the gent at that position with whom they link up, arms
                around each other's backs.

                The four new couples lead around anti-clockwise in six bars
                until they return to the gents original places.   8 bars

D CIRCLE   All dancers face to the centre, joining hands in a circle, and
                advance to the centre and retire, twice.   8 bars

E SWING   All four couples (gents in their original places and with new
                partners) swing in place.   8 bars

F REPEAT   Repeat C to E.
                The four ladies move on one place again.   24 bars

G REPEAT   Repeat C to E.
                The four ladies move on one place again.   24 bars

H REPEAT   Repeat C to E.
                The four ladies return to their original partners.   24 bars

The Cuil Aodha Set

LEARNED IN DUBLIN FROM TIM DENNEHY AND JOE O'DONOVAN.

A DIFFERENT VERSION IS DANCED IN KNOCKNAGREE.

THE CUIL AODHA SET

'Wheel'

Opening Position: All four couples join hands in front and face anti-clockwise around the circle, gents on the inside

A LEAD AROUND   All four couples dance anti-clockwise around until back in original places.   8 bars

B FIGURE   WHEEL: Each top couple turns to face the side couple to their left.

Each group of four dancers, 1st tops & 1st sides, and 2nd tops & 2nd sides, join right hands in the centre and dance clockwise for four bars, then turn, join left hands in centre and dance anti-clockwise for four bars.   8 bars

C BODY   Couples adopt the standard position.

All four couples dance together one bar into the centre and one bar back to their own positions. They then dance two bars around to the position of the couple to their right, turning clockwise as they go.

The four couples repeat this movement three more times until they end up back in their starting positions.   16 bars

D HOUSE   All four couples dance house around.   8 bars

E LEAD AROUND   Repeat A.   8 bars

F FIGURE   Repeat B.   On this occasion the side couples turn to the top couples to their left.   8 bars

G BODY   Repeat C.   16 bars

H HOUSE   All four couples dance house around.   8 bars

THE CUIL AODHA SET

'Ladies In'

Polka - 104 bars

Opening Position: All four couples join hands in front and face anti-clockwise around the circle, gents on the inside.

A LEAD   All four couples dance anti-clockwise around until back in original
  AROUND   places.   8 bars

B FIGURE (a) LADIES IN: Each gent holds his partners right hand in his right hand. While the gents dance in place their partners dance past in front of them, turning anti-clockwise, until all the ladies are back-to-back in the centre facing out. (see page 85)

They then dance back out past their partners, still turning anti-clockwise, until they are back on the outside again.

The gents' right arms should now be around the ladies shoulders, still holding the ladies right hands in their right hands.

Gents take the ladies' left hands in their left hands.   4 bars

(b) LEAD AROUND: All four couples lead half-way around to the opposite places.   4 bars

(c) LADIES IN: The four ladies dance into the centre and back out again, as in (a). On this occasion they dance in turning clockwise. They dance back out turning anti-clockwise, as above.   4 bars

(d) LEAD AROUND: All four couples lead half-way around back to their own places again.   4 bars

C BODY   All   four   couples   dance   the   Body,   as   in   figure 1. 16 bars

D HOUSE   All four couples dance house around.   8 bars

E LEAD
  AROUND   Repeat A.   8 bars

F FIGURE   Repeat B.   8 bars

G BODY   All four couples dance the Body.   16 bars

H HOUSE   All four couples dance house around.   8 bars

THE CUIL AODHA SET

'Swing'

Polka - 96 bars

Opening Position: All four couples join hands in front and face anti-clockwise around the circle, gents on the inside.

A LEAD AROUND — All four couples dance anti-clockwise around until back in original places. — 8 bars

B FIGURE (a) SWING: The couples seperate. Each dancer turns away from their own partner to the nearest gent to their right (ladies) or lady to their left (gents), and swings with them. — 8 bars

(b) SWING: The original couples re-form and swing in place. — 8 bars

C BODY — All four couples dance the Body, as in figure 1. — 16 bars

D HOUSE — All four couples dance house around. — 8 bars

E FIGURE — Repeat B. — 16 bars

F BODY — All four couples dance the Body. — 16 bars

G HOUSE — All four couples dance house around. — 8 bars

THE CUIL AODHA SET

'Side Step'

4th Figure

Polka - 80 bars

Opening Position: All four couples join hands in front and face anti-clockwise around the circle, gents on the inside.

A LEAD AROUND — All couples dance anti-clockwise around until back in original places. — 8 bars

B FIGURE — SIDESTEP: All couples face to centre, standing side by side.

Ladies side step to left, in front of their partners, who side step to the right. Ladies and gents end up in each others places (2 bars).

All dance in place (2 bars).

They all side-step back to own places (2 bars), gents in front, and dance in place, (2 bars). — 8 bars

C BODY — All four couples dance the Body, as in figure 1. — 16 bars

D HOUSE — All four couples dance house around. — 8 bars

E FIGURE — Repeat B. — 8 bars

F BODY — All four couples dance the Body. — 16 bars

G HOUSE — All four couples dance house around. — 8 bars

57

THE CUIL AODHA SET

'Chain'

Opening Position: All four couples join hands in front and face anti-clockwise around the circle, gents on the inside.

A	LEAD AROUND	All four couples dance anti-clockwise around until back in original places.	8 bars
B	FIGURE (a)	CHAIN: Each couple holds right hands, gents facing anti-clockwise and ladies clockwise around the circle. Each couple dances around each other in place once, and then the couples seperate and each person dances off in the direction they are facing, giving their left hands to the dancer coming towards them, and then right, left etc. until they meet their own partners half way around the circle.	8 bars
	(b)	SWING: All four couples, who are now at opposite sides of the circle from their starting positions, swing in place.	8 bars
C	BODY	All four couples dance the Body, as in figure 1.	16 bars
D	HOUSE	All four couples dance house around.	8 bars
E	FIGURE	Repeat B. Each couple ends up back in their original position and swings there.	16 bars
F	BODY	All four couples dance the Body.	16 bars
G	HOUSE	All four couples dance house around.	8 bars

THE CUIL AODHA SET

'Big Wheel'

6th Figure   Polka - 120 bars

Opening Position: All four couples join hands in front and face anti-clockwise
around the circle, gents on the inside.

A LEAD
AROUND
     All four couples dance anti-clockwise around until back in original
places.   8 bars

B FIGURE (a) LADIES CIRCLE: The four ladies join hands forming a circle and
dance into the centre and out again twice.   8 bars

       (b) WHEEL: The four gents join right hands in centre and dance four
bars around clockwise, then turn (clockwise), join left hands in
centre and dance four bars anti-clockwise back to their own
places.   8 bars

          Gents do not release hands or stop dancing but pick up their part-
ners by placing their right arms around their waists, then wheel
around with them until back in place. (see page 82)   8 bars

C BODY   All four couples dance the Body, as in figure 1.   16 bars

D HOUSE   All four couples dance house around.   8 bars

E LEAD
AROUND   Repeat A.   8 bars

F FIGURE   Repeat B.   24 bars

G BODY   All four couples dance the Body.   16 bars

H HOUSE   All four couples dance house around.   8 bars

The Sliabh Luachra Set

LEARNED IN DAN O'CONNELL'S PUBLIC HOUSE IN KNOCKNAGREE, AND IN SCARTA-GLEN, DURING THE AUGUST BANK HOLIDAY WEEKEND OF 1983. IN KNOCKNAGREE THIS SET IS CALLED SIMPLY A 'POLKA SET' IT IS OFTEN REFERRED TO, OUTSIDE KERRY, AS THE KNOCKNAGREE SET. IN VIEW OF THE FACT THAT IT IS NOT CON-FINED TO KNOCKNAGREE, AND TO DISTIN-GUISH IT FROM THE OTHER POLKA SETS I HAVE CALLED IT THE SLIABH LUACHRA SET HERE.

I AM INDEBTED TO DAN O'CONNELL AND HIS WIFE, AND TO HIS NEIGHBOURS AND CUSTOMERS FOR THE EXTRAORDINARILY WARM HOSPITALITY AND FRIENDSHIP EXTENDED TO MY WIFE AND MYSELF WHEN WE VISITED KNOCKNAGREE TO LEARN THIS SET.

THE SLIABH LUACHRA SET

'Ladies Chain'

1st Figure   Polka - 96 bars

Opening Position: Couples adopt the standard position.

A **BODY**   All four couples dance together one bar into the centre and one
                    bar back to their own places. They then dance two bars around to
                    the position of the couple to their right, turning clockwise as they
                    go.

                    The four couples repeat the movement three more times until they
                    end up back in their starting positions.   16 bars

B **FIGURE** (a) **LADIES CHAIN:**   TOP LADIES dance to centre, chain with right
                    hands and pass each other, give left hands to opposite gents and
                    dance around them, the gents turning with the ladies, dance to the
                    centre again, chain with right hands and pass each other to return
                    to their partners.   8 bars

              (b) **SWING:**   TOP COUPLES swing in place.   8 bars

C **BODY**   All four couples dance the Body.   16 bars

D **FIGURE**   SIDE COUPLES repeat B.   16 bars

E **BODY**   All four couples dance the Body.   16 bars

F **HOUSE**   All four couples dance house around.   8 bars

61

THE SLIABH LUACHRA SET

'Show The Lady'

2nd Figure

Polka - 160 bars

Opening Position: Couples adopt the standard position.

A BODY   All four couples dance the Body as in figure 1.   16 bars

B FIGURE (a) HOUSE: 1ST TOPS dance around the house inside.   8 bars

         (b) HOME: 1ST TOPS side-step into the centre (1 bar), and dance on the spot (1 bar); side-step back to their position (1 bar), and dance on the spot, (1 bar); then dance around at home (4 bars). 8 bars

C BODY   All four couples dance the Body.   16 bars

D FIGURE   HOUSE & HOME: 1ST SIDES repeat B.   16 bars

E BODY   All four couples dance the Body.   16 bars

F FIGURE   HOUSE & HOME: 2ND TOPS repeat B.   16 bars

G BODY   All four couples dance the Body.   16 bars

H FIGURE   HOUSE & HOME: 2ND SIDES repeat B.   16 bars

I BODY   All four couples dance the Body.   16 bars

J HOUSE   All four couples dance house around.   8 bars

'In, Out and Roundabout'

3rd Figure   Jig - 160 bars

Opening Position: Couples adopt the standard position.

A BODY   All four couples dance the Body as in figure 1.   16 bars

B FIGURE   (a) SLIDE: TOP COUPLES side-step towards each other in the centre
               (2 bars), and then side-step back to their own positions (2 bars).   4 bars

           (b) CHANGE: TOP COUPLES dance half-way around the fringe to
               each other's position.   4 bars

           (c) SLIDE: TOP COUPLES repeat (a).   4 bars

           (d) CHANGE: TOP COUPLES repeat (b) to bring them back to their
               own positions again.   4 bars

C BODY   All four couples dance the Body.   16 bars

D FIGURE   SLIDE & CHANGE: SIDE COUPLES repeat B.   16 bars

E BODY   All four couples dance the Body,   16 bars

F FIGURE   SLIDE & CHANGE: TOP COUPLES repeat B.   16 bars

G BODY   All four couples dance the Body.   16 bars

H FIGURE   SLIDE & CHANGE: SIDE COUPLES repeat B.   16 bars

I BODY   All four couples dance the Body.   16 bars

J HOUSE   All four couples dance house around.   8 bars

63

THE SLIABH LUACHRA SET

'Around The House & Mind The Dresser'

4th Figure   Polka - 72 bars

Opening Position:	All four couples hold hands in front and face anti-clockwise around the circle, gents on the inside.	
A LEAD AROUND	All four couples dance anti-clockwise around until back in their original places.	8 bars
B FIGURE (a)	TURN THE LADY: All the gents take their partners right hands and turn their partners under their right arms four times, while dancing in place themselves.	
	The ladies turn in a clockwise direction.	8 bars
(b)	LADIES RIGHT HANDS IN: The four ladies join right hands in the centre and wheel clockwise half-way around to the opposite gent.	
	Each lady links left elbows with the opposite gent's left elbow and dances around him twice, the gents turning with the ladies.	
	The four ladies then join right hands in the centre again and wheel clockwise around back to their own partners.	8 bars
C SWING	All four couples swing in place.	8 bars
D LEAD AROUND	All four couples repeat A.	8 bars
E FIGURE	Repeat B.	16 bars
F SWING	All four couples swing in place.	8 bars

THE SLIABH LUACHRA SET

Opening Position:	Couples about to dance adopt the standard position. Top couples dance the figure first while side couples leave the floor. When the tops finish they leave the floor and sides take up position. Sides are followed in the same way by tops again, and then finally sides again to finish. No more than 8 bars should be allowed to go by while the couples take up position.	

A <u>FIGURE</u> (a) <u>HOUSE:</u> TOP COUPLES dance house around.   **8 bars**

(b) <u>SLIDE & CHANGE:</u> Top couples side-step into the centre (2 bars), and then side-step back to their own positions (2 bars).

They then dance half-way around the house to each other's position (4 bars).

This whole movement is then repeated to bring them back to their own positions again.   **16 bars**

(c) <u>HOUSE:</u> TOP COUPLES dance house around.   **8 bars**

(d) <u>SLIDE & CHANGE:</u> TOP COUPLES repeat (b).   **16 bars**

(e) <u>HOUSE:</u> TOP COUPLES dance house around.   **8 bars**

B <u>FIGURE</u>   SIDE COUPLES take the floor and repeat A.   **56 bars**

C <u>FIGURE</u>   TOP COUPLES take the floor and repeat A.   **56 bars**

D <u>FIGURE</u>   SIDE COUPLES take the floor and repeat A.   **56 bars**

6th Figure   Hornpipe - 160 bars

Opening Position: Couples adopt the standard position.

A BODY   All four couples dance the Body as in figure 1.   16 bars

B HOUSE   All four couples dance house around.   8 bars

C CHANGE   While the gents stand in place, the four ladies leave their part-
  PARTNERS   ners and move around to take up the opening position with the
                next gent to their right.   This movement is not danced.   8 bars

D BODY   All four couples dance the Body.   16 bars

E HOUSE   All four couples dance house around.   8 bars

F CHANGE   Repeat C.   8 bars
  PARTNERS

G BODY   All four couples dance the Body.   16 bars

H HOUSE   All four couples dance house around.   8 bars

I CHANGE   Repeat C   8 bars
  PARTNERS

J BODY   All four couples dance the Body.   16 bars

K HOUSE   All four couples dance house around.   8 bars

L CHANGE   Repeat C to bring all the ladies back to their original partners
  PARTNERS   again.   8 bars

M BODY   All four couples dance the Body.   16 bars

N HOUSE   All four couples dance house around.   8 bars

66

The Steps

A knowledge of the appropriate steps for each set or figure is indispensable for complete enjoyment of the dances, and it also produces a pleasing visual effect for onlookers. It is not suggested that every dancer should perform every movement in exactly the same way. In fact a great deal of the pleasure to be derived from watching many sets comes from the manner in which some traditional dancers introduce idiosyncratic movements and variations into their stepping. But this can only be done if everyone stays within a general framework. The sequence in which the feet are used must obviously be such as to facilitate movement around the floor. Less obviously, the rhythmic pattern beaten out by the feet on the floor must be in accord with the type of tune to which one is dancing. Within these constraints considerable improvisation is possible. The rhythm essential to good dancing may only be acquired through tuition and observation. It is possible however, to indicate in written form how the various steps are constructed, and it is this basic information that follows here. It must be realised that familiarity with the steps as shown here should be regarded as merely a starting point in learning them.

In the following instructions the capital letters "R" and "L" refer to right and left foot. If the "R" or "L" is underline{followed} by a lower case "t" it indicates that the toe should be used. Do not try to dance too far forwards on the toe; the ball of the foot is more what is intended. If the "R" or "L" is underline{followed} by a lower case "h" the action required of the dancer is that he or she, having the toe of the foot in question already in contact with the floor, simply bring the heel down as well so that the whole foot is flat on the floor. The dancer should not have his or her heel on the floor with the toe raised from it.
If the "R" or "L" is underline{preceded} by a "h", "k", "c" or "s" (lower case), it indicates that the foot is used to perform a particular action, as follows:

"h" means that the dancer should hop so as to come down on the foot indicated on the beat of the music.

"k" stands for "kick", and means that the foot in question should be kicked out in front (but not too far or high).

"c" stands for "cut", and means that the foot should be raised slightly and the leg bent at the knee to cross the raised leg over the other one, the toe pointing down.

"s" means that the foot should be stamped down on the beat of the music.

The most important thing to take care with when learning steps is to have the weight on the correct foot at all times.   Where the letter or set of letters is underlined it means that the dancer's weight should be placed on the foot at that point.   Otherwise the foot should tap the floor and be raised again, unless some other action is indicated, such as the "kick" and the "cut" where the foot does not touch the floor at all.

Readers unfamiliar with music should regard the notes in the instructions below as merely a means of counting out the time, all the notes shown in any line occupying exactly the same amount of time. The beat of the music in each case comes on the first note of each group of four (in the case of reels and hornpipes), of three (in the case of jigs and slides) or of two (in the case of polkas).

It should also be noted that in Irish dance tunes a phrase of the melody does not coincide with a whole number of full bars.   A coherent phrase will usually include one or two notes of the preceding bar, a number of full bars, and finally an incomplete bar, leaving the final notes to be included in the following phrase, as follows:

The Gold Ring (1st four bars)

It is for this reason that one sees introductory notes before the first bar of most printed versions of dance tunes.   Dancing follows the phrases of the music rather than the full bars as they are formally written down, and a full step should be thought of as including the movement before the bar-line.   This will be seen in the examples on the following pages.

1   REEL STEP - ADVANCE

| LADIES | Lh | Rt | Rh | Lt | Lh | Rt | Lt | Rt | Rh |
| GENTS | Rh | Lt | Lh | Rt | Rh | Lt | Rt | Lt | Lh |

2   REEL STEP - RETIRE

| LADIES | Rh | Lt | Lh | Rt | Rh | Lt | Rt | Lt | Lh |
| GENTS | Lh | Rt | Rh | Lt | Lh | Rt | Lt | Rt | Rh |

3   REEL STEP - DANCE AROUND (House, Home & Lead/Wheel Around)

| LADIES | Lh | Rt | Lt | Rt | Rh | Lt | Rt | Lt | Lh |
| GENTS | Rh | Lt | Rt | Lt | Lh | Rt | Lt | Rt | Rh |

4   REEL STEP - DANCE AROUND (Doubled)

| LADIES | Lh | Rt | Lt | Rt | Lt |
| GENTS | Rh | Lt | Rt | Lt | Rt |

5   REEL STEP - GALWAY SET

| LADIES | hL | Rt | Rt | Lt | Lt | Rt | Rt | hR | Lt | Lt | Rt | Rt | Lt | Lt |
| GENTS | hR | Lt | Lt | Rt | Rt | Lt | Lt | hL | Rt | Rt | Lt | Lt | Rt | Rt |

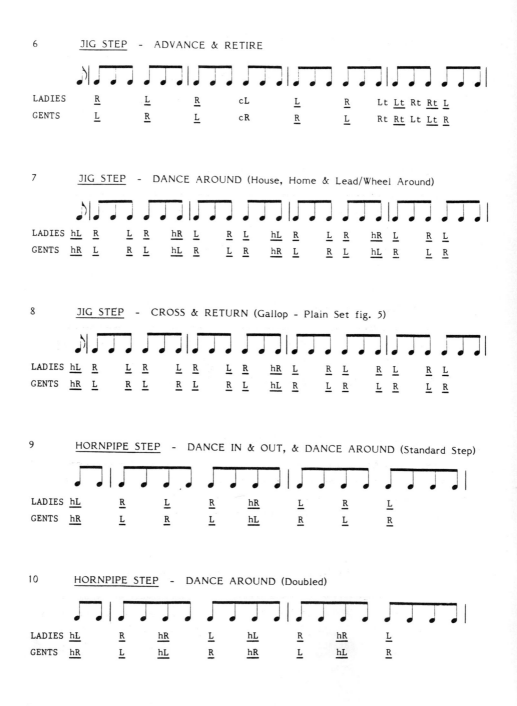

6   JIG STEP - ADVANCE & RETIRE

LADIES	R	L	R	cL	L	R	Lt	Lt Rt Rt	L
GENTS	L	R	L	cR	R	L	Rt	Rt Lt Lt	R

7   JIG STEP - DANCE AROUND (House, Home & Lead/Wheel Around)

LADIES	hL	R	L	R	hR	L	R	L	hL	R	L	R	hR	L	R	L
GENTS	hR	L	R	L	hL	R	L	R	hR	L	R	L	hL	R	L	R

8   JIG STEP - CROSS & RETURN (Gallop - Plain Set fig. 5)

LADIES	hL	R	L	R	L	R	L	R	hR	L	R	L	R	L	R	L
GENTS	hR	L	R	L	R	L	R	L	hL	R	L	R	L	R	L	R

9   HORNPIPE STEP - DANCE IN & OUT, & DANCE AROUND (Standard Step)

LADIES	hL	R	L	R	hR	L	R	L
GENTS	hR	L	R	L	hL	R	L	R

10   HORNPIPE STEP - DANCE AROUND (Doubled)

LADIES	hL	R	hR	L	hL	R	hR	L
GENTS	hR	L	hL	R	hR	L	hL	R

70

11 HORNPIPE STEP - DANCE IN & OUT (Kerry Set)

LADIES	hL	R	L	R	sL	L	R	L
GENTS	hR	L	R	L	sR	R	L	R

12 HORNPIPE STEP - DANCE IN/ADVANCE (Monaghan Set)

LADIES	hL	R	L	R	kL	L	R	L	kR
GENTS	hR	L	R	L	kR	R	L	R	kL

13 HORNPIPE STEP - DANCE OUT/RETIRE (Monaghan Set)

LADIES	kR	Rt	Rh	Lt	Lh	Rt	Rh	L
GENTS	kL	Lt	Lh	Rt	Rh	Lt	Lh	R

14 HORNPIPE STEP - CASTLE LFT (Clap & Stamp)

LADIES		clap	clap	clap	hR	L	R	L
GENTS		clap	clap	clap	hR	L	R	R

15 POLKA STEP - BASIC   POLKA STEP - ALTERNATIVE

LADIES	R	L	R	L	R	L	R	R	L	R	L	L	R	L
GENTS	L	R	L	R	L	R	L	L	R	L	R	R	L	R

SLIDE STEP

The typical note-group of a slide is a crochet , followed by a quaver, this group occuring twice in a bar. It may be thought of as a double jig played so rapidly that passing notes have to be excluded and only the accented notes, on and off the beat, are played. The difference between the slide's long and short note, and the polka's accented and unaccented note may appear slight, but is quite marked when heard.

The following example consists of the first four bars of a typical slide, "Merrily Kiss The Quaker". It will be noticed that the afore-mentioned "typical" note-group occurs only twice, out of a possible eight occurrences. The second and third lines show how the melody and rhythm may be simplified to its typical basic structure. In the fourth line each crochet has been divided into two quavers in order to show a line with all possible beats against which to set the steps.

Comparison of this step with steps 7 and 15 above will show that it lies between those two steps while differing from both. An interesting and instructive exercise is to dance steps 3, 9, 7, 16 and 15 (i.e. the basic reel, hornpipe, jig, slide and polka steps) in that order, or the reverse. The relationship between the various different steps will be seen if this is done.

16   <u>SLIDE STEP</u> - DANCE IN & OUT, & DANCE AROUND (Standard Step)

The Music

Music that is suitable for set dancing should have a pronounced rhythm and a not too complicated structure. The following five pieces of music are good examples of what is required, each one a good representative of its type. Few, if any, set dance figures are danced to measures other than the five included here.

All five tunes are taken from Breandán Breathnach's collection 'Ceol Rince na hEireann' Vol. ii.

Reel   **C.R.É. ii 208(i)**

Jig   **C.R.É. ii 18**

Hornpipe   **C.R.É. ii 301**

Polka   C.R.É. ii 108

Slide   C.R.É. ii 77

Glossary Of Terms

ADVANCE: Used in Reel figures. When one or more dancers, in a line or circle, dance straight forwards without turning.

ANTI-CLOCKWISE: The terms "anti-clockwise" and "clockwise" are used here to describe turning movements, either of an individual or couple in place, or of dancers around the floor, as they would be seen from above.

ARCH: This movement occurs here only in the last figure of the Mazurka set. Two dancers face each other, take each other's hands and raise them so as to allow other dancers to pass under.

BODY: A particular sequence of movements that is repeated during a figure, between the particular movements that characterise that figure. See the Kerry Set.

CHAIN: When two or more dancers form two "streams" dancing in opposite directions, usually in the form of a circle, they weave left and right, joining right and left hands alternately with the dancers approaching them.

CHANGE: Used here in reel figures to indicate that couples should exchange places.
See also "ladies change", "gents change" and "change partners".

CHANGE PARTNERS: Indicates any movement where dancers leave their original partners for new ones.

CHRISTMAS: "Big Christmas" and "Little Christmas" refer respectively to eight or four dancers forming a tight circle facing inwards, arms behind each other's backs and side-stepping around.

CIRCLE: Eight or four dancers joining hands and facing into the centre.

CLOCKWISE: See "anti-clockwise".

CROSS: Refers here to a dancer dancing straight, rather than diagonally, across to the opposite lady or gent, or back to their own partner, without turning.

DOUBLE: See section on steps (reel and hornpipe).   Usually at the end of a figure dancers will simplify the step, enabling them to change feet twice as often during a bar.   The couple has to turn faster, and this imparts a flourish to the end of a figure.

FACE THE WALL: The name of the 6th figure of the Mazurka Set.

FIGURE: The term "figure" is applied to the individual dances which comprise the set, and also to the characteristic movements within each of these dances that distinguish them from others in the same set.   The manner in which the movements in each figure have been designated the "figure" (in the second sense) here is quite arbitrary. The object in each case was to devise an easily remembered structure for each figure.

GALLOP: See the fifth figure of the Plain Set, and the section on steps.

GENTS IN: The four gents advance to the centre together.

HANDS AROUND: Name used in the Kerry Set for the "wheel" movement.

HIGH GATES: Name of the third figure of the Mazurka Set.

HOME: See diagrams.   The area of the dance floor immediately around each couple.

HOUSE: "House around" or "house inside" refer respectively to one or more couples dancing anti-clockwise around within the circle formed by the four couples, or around the line of the circle.   See diagrams.

LADIES CHAIN: Chain movement in which the ladies alone participate.

LADIES CHANGE: Opposite ladies exchange places.

LADIES CIRCLE: The four ladies join hands in a circle facing into the centre.

LADIES IN: The four ladies advance to the centre together.

LADIES LEFT HAND CHAIN: Ladies chain started with left hands.

LADIES RIGHT HAND CHAIN: Ladies chain started with right hands.

LADIES RIGHT HANDS IN: Wheel movement performed by ladies only, in a clockwise direction.

LEAD AROUND: Movement in which a couple dance forward side-by-side around a circular path, either inside the set, when one or two couples are performing it, or around the line of the circle when all couples are performing it.
When leading around the lady and gent can join hands in front, or the gent can place his right arm over his partners shoulder or around her back to take the lady's right hand, (or vice versa for leading around clockwise).   Whatever the direction the gent should be on the inside.   See diagrams.

LINE UP: Movement in the fifth figure of the Lancers Set.

PASS BY: Movement in the second figure of the Lancers Set.

PASS THROUGH: Movement in which two couples dance towards each other and pass with either one couple going between the opposing dancers, as in the Monaghan Set, or the gents passing on the outside and the ladies on the inside, as in the Plain and Galway Sets.

RETIRE: As in "advance & retire".   A dancer or couple or line (straight or circular) dances backwards to return to a position from which they have just danced forwards.

SIDES: The "sides" or "side couples" are two couples facing each other side-on to the source of the music.   They are last to perform each figure.   See diagrams.

SIDESTEP: Step used for dancing sideways in either direction. The term is also applied to the movement or figure in which the step is employed.

SLIDE: A type of tune in 6/8 time and the dance associated with it.   The tune may be thought of as a double jig speeded up and simplified in structure to give a more strongly accented effect. See also the diagrams and steps.

SLIDE (REEL):   In reel figures here the term "slide" is used to describe the movement of a couple from their home position to the centre and back again.   This can be done in the standard hold either with both dancers facing half to the front, or with the gent facing forwards and the lady backwards and to the right of the gent, or the couple may face full forwards, arms behind each other's backs.

SQUARE: In the first figure of the Lancers Set the couples dancing around inside should travel along a square rather than a circle.

STANDARD HOLD: The "waltz" hold.

SWING: The term "swing" is used here to describe a movement that has at least one other name. It is a movement in which a couple turn rapidly while dancing in place. The step is the simplest possible, with both the lady's and gent's right foot coming down on the beat of the music, and left foot, which is used to propel the dancer around, off the beat. Both dancers should face past each other, in the direction of the movement.

If the couple keep their right feet in an instep-to-instep position less floor space will be used and a neater effect achieved. There are three holds used for the swing. The standard hold is completely adequate and is recommended. Fumbling for other holds often disrupts the flow of the dance.

The other holds are first, the lady and gent place their right hands around each other's waists and join left hands, and second, the lady and gent join right hands, holding them at chest level, and with their left hands grip their partner's right elbows.

THREES: In certain figures a line or circle of three dancers is formed to perform a movement.

TOPS: The "tops" or "top couples" are two couples facing each other, one facing the music (1st tops) and the other with backs to the music (2nd tops). They are first to perform each figure.

TURN THE LADY: Movement in which a couple join right hands and the lady dances in place while turning clockwise under the gent's raised arm. The gent should also dance in place during this movement.

WHEEL: Movement in which gents, ladies or couples join left or right hands at a central point and dance around a circular path, all facing the same way, the arms forming the spokes of the "wheel".

Illustrations

The following illustrations should be used in conjunction with the text to work out the positions and movements involved in the various figures. The dancers' orientation can be worked out from the fact that each right arm is shown in white and each left arm in black, and ladies and represented by a circle and gents by a square. In each illustration 1st tops couple occupy the top position.

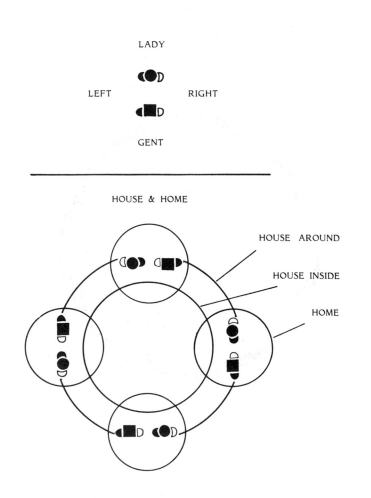

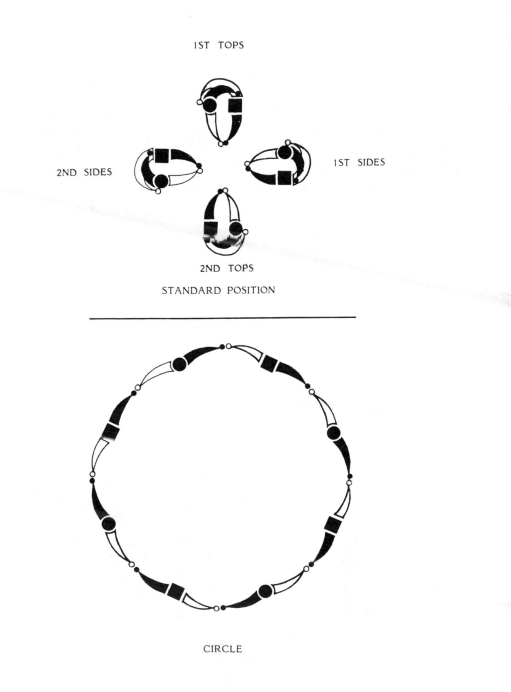

1ST TOPS

2ND SIDES

1ST SIDES

2ND TOPS

STANDARD POSITION

CIRCLE

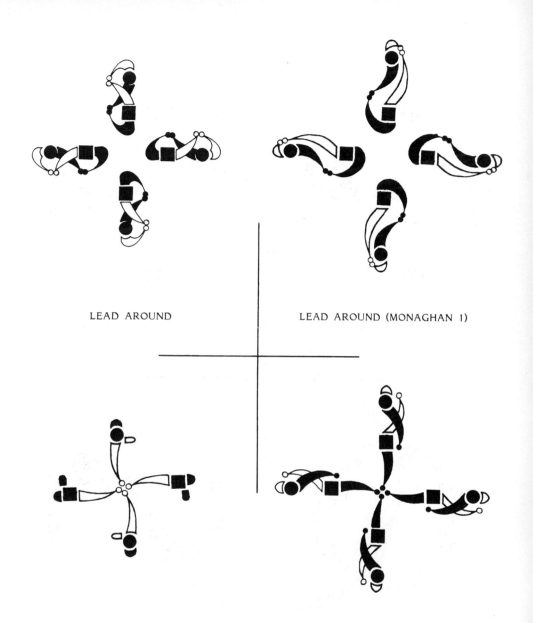

LEAD AROUND

LEAD AROUND (MONAGHAN 1)

WHEEL

WHEEL [CUIL AODHA - 6 B. (b)]

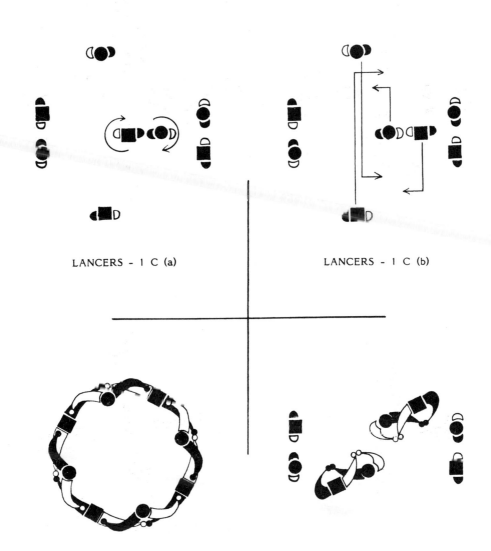

LANCERS - 1 C (a)

LANCERS - 1 C (b)

LANCERS - 3 C (e)

LANCERS - 4 C (b)

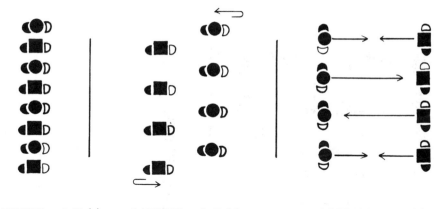

LANCERS - 5 C (a)   LANCERS - 5 C (b)   LANCERS - 5 C (d)

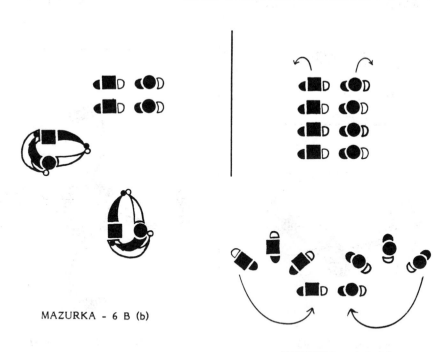

MAZURKA - 6 B (b)

MAZURKA - 6 B (c)

84

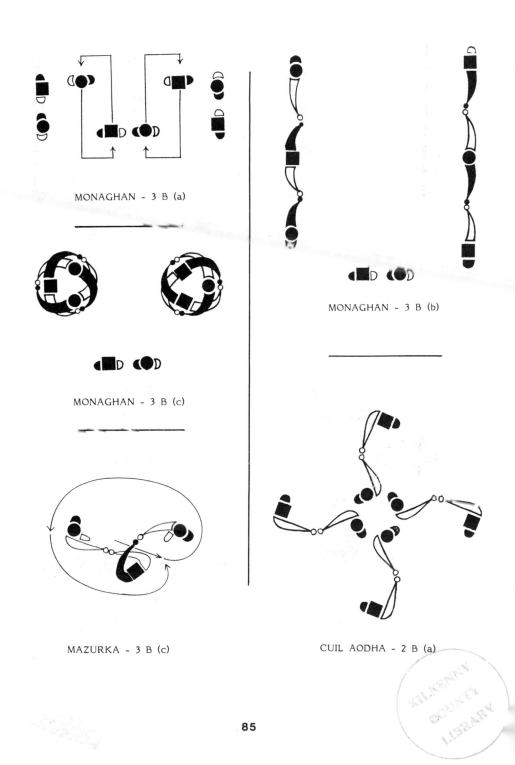

MONAGHAN - 3 B (a)

MONAGHAN - 3 B (b)

MONAGHAN - 3 B (c)

MAZURKA - 3 B (c)

CUIL AODHA - 2 B (a)

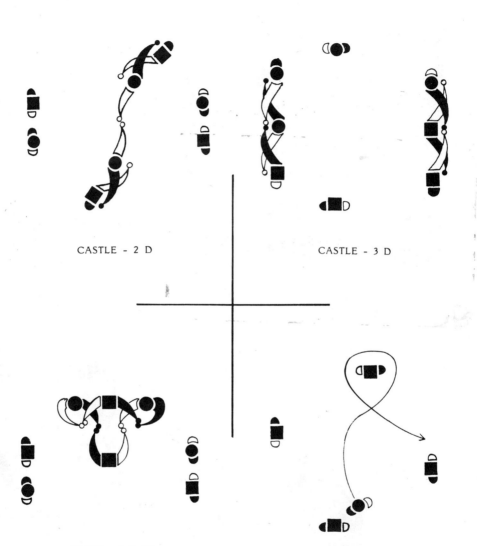

CASTLE - 2 D

CASTLE - 3 D

PLAIN - 3 C (d)

PLAIN - 5 D (b)
(PATH TAKEN BY EACH LADY)